C000058881

THE POCKET BOOK OF
ANGELS

THE POCKET BOOK OF
ANGELS

*The power of a protective
presence in your life*

Arcturus

ARCTURUS

This edition published in 2015 by Arcturus Publishing Limited
26/27 Bickels Yard, 151–153 Bermondsey Street,
London SE1 3HA

ISBN: 978-1-78404-564-7
AD004468UK

Printed in China

Contents

The Angelic Realm

> *Every visible thing in this world*
> *is put in the charge of an angel.*
>
> St. Augustine

From the east to the west sped those angels of the Dawn, from sea to sea, from mountain-top to mountain-top, scattering light from breast and wing.

H. Rider Haggard

Their wings betoken their coming to mankind as messengers, but their haloes symbolize that they come from heaven, which is their home.

Mortimer J. Adler

*All arrangements that are carried out between
heaven and earth are carried out through angels.*

Mirza Ghulam Ahmad

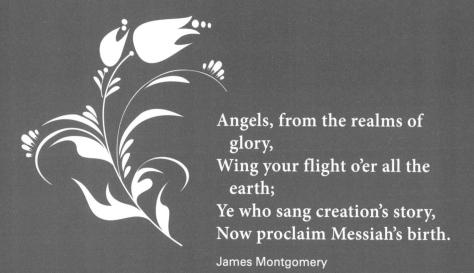

Angels, from the realms of
    glory,
Wing your flight o'er all the
    earth;
Ye who sang creation's story,
Now proclaim Messiah's birth.

James Montgomery

**What know we of
the Blest above
But that they sing,
and that they love?**

William Wordsworth

'FOLLOW ME...'

In 1994, my mother – who has a history of heart problems – and father were about to drive over two hundred miles back home from Las Vegas. Once in the car, my mother had a difficult time breathing, and it appeared that she would not live through the four-hour journey home. Suddenly a Hispanic woman drove up and told my father to follow her and she would guide him to the nearest hospital.

The woman drove through Las Vegas like she had every street memorized. When they arrived at the hospital, the woman walked into the emergency room and began to give orders like she was a doctor on the staff. My mother was wheeled into the emergency room and the woman consoled her, assuring her that everything would be fine. When my father turned round to thank her, the woman was already in her car, driving away from the hospital.

My father got the license plate number on her car and gave it to my brother, who was an attorney, to investigate, so that he and my mother could find out her name and address and formally thank her. My brother wrote to the State of Nevada Department of Motor Vehicles, requesting the information.

They told him that no such license plate number existed.

That companion speedily conducts the man who is devoted to duty and effaces his sins by austerities, to the next world, radiant and clothed with an ethereal body.

Manavadharmashastra

There are celestial bodies and there are terrestrial bodies; but the glory of the celestial is one, and the glory of the terrestrial is another.

Corinthians 15.35-44

The huge dragon, the ancient serpent, who is called the Devil and Satan, who deceived the whole world, was thrown down to earth, and its angels were thrown down with it.

Revelation 12:7-9

GLEAMING LIKE THE SUN

The day after my great-grandmother's funeral, my uncle took a picture of the setting sun. On the picture, where the sun and its rays were, was a bright and brilliant full angel. Comprised of the sun's rays, as you would see them in any picture or video, the angel appeared in a range of reds, blues, purples and oranges. It was stunning.

The sun was where the angel's face would have been. The angel's wings were gleaming pink and she had long robes, perfectly symmetrical; there were no legs or arms, it was simply one solid 'dress shape', like a snow angel. This picture has hung in the hall of my aunt's house in loving memory of my great-grandmother ever since. I have a feeling she is watching out for all of us.

The angels in the celestial kingdom have vastly more knowledge and wisdom than the angels in the spiritual kingdom. The celestial angels do not think and speak from faith, like the spiritual angels, but from an internal perception that a thing is so.

Emanuel Swedenborg

Those clouds are angels' robes. —That fiery west
Is paved with smiling faces.

Charles Kingsley

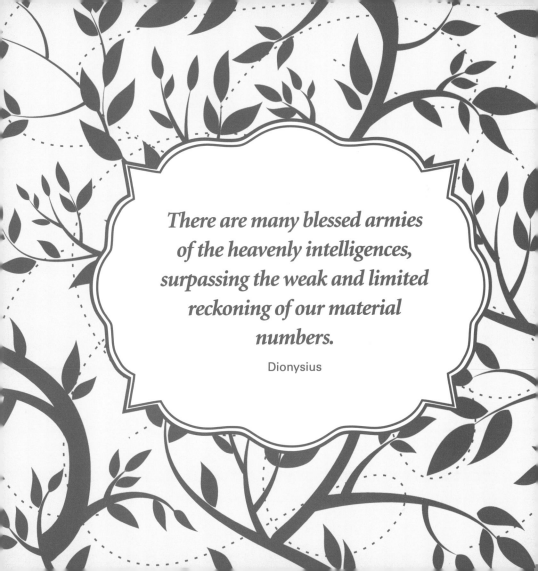

There are many blessed armies of the heavenly intelligences, surpassing the weak and limited reckoning of our material numbers.

Dionysius

OUT-OF-BODY EXPERIENCE

While in a deep sleep, I heard someone call my name. I sat up because it almost sounded as though it had been a shout. I saw a young man, who looked very familiar, with brown wavy hair and green eyes. There was a deep light coming from within him that made his being shine and lit my room. It didn't frighten me. He stood as though on solid ground, but he wasn't touching the floor. He was dressed in a white, robe-like garment. I looked behind me and saw that I had sat up out of my body, which was still lying in the bed.

The visitor held out his hand and beckoned me to take his. He communicated by thought; there was no movement of his mouth when he conversed with me. I felt what he said in my heart.

So I took his hand and, in an instant, we traveled by thought, appearing above and to the side of each of my

family members' beds. He spoke of events and situations that had occurred in the past, and what was happening now, and where it all would lead in the future. Then he showed me where, when and how I was to intervene.

The things he told me I still carry with me, but they only come to me when the time and situation is perfect. He told me this was the way it would be, because what he shared would overwhelm me if I were to remember all of it at once.

Since then many things have happened, and I somehow know exactly what to do, and how and what to say. And I know where it's coming from. In a way, for a long time, I felt I had been robbed of my free agency to choose. But time is proving me wrong. I am glad for my experience and will always be thankful that someone cared enough to warn and help my family.

When it is said that all things, even the angels, would lapse into nothing unless preserved by God, it is not to be gathered therefrom that there is any principle of corruption in the angels; but that the nature of the angels is dependent upon God as its cause.

St. Thomas Aquinas

In their role
as celestial servants to
humans on earth, Angels
act variously as guardians,
guides, teachers, truth-givers
and comforters, protectors of
the righteous, punishers of
the wicked, and more.

David Connolly

'I DIDN'T WANT THEM TO LEAVE...'

I was 16 and started getting sick at school and couldn't keep anything down. I went into hospital, as my symptoms got worse. I had surgery and they removed stones from my gall-bladder and took out my appendix. I woke up in intensive care and realized I had been put there due to complications during the surgery.

A few days later I was moved to progressive care. I was having difficulties recovering from the surgery. The next morning, two young men dressed in white came into my room and said, 'Good morning, Paul. We will be taking care of you today.' They spent the whole day with me. I sensed there was something different about these two men; they were so completely kind and caring and I seemed to be drawn to them somehow! There was almost a glow in their faces and they never complained and were completely devoted to my care. I had never had anyone give me that much attention and they were so loving in

everything they did! Towards the end of the day they told me 'good-bye' and said I wouldn't be in the hospital much longer. I didn't want them to leave!

The next morning, a nurse came in to take my vital signs and I asked if the two young men who had taken care of me were still there. The nurse looked perplexed and said, 'There weren't two young men working in this unit yesterday. I came into your room several times to check on you and didn't see them here.'

Those two young men were right – it wasn't long before I was discharged. I'll never forget my two wonderful angels and the help, care and love they bestowed on me that day.

A demon holds a book in which are written the sins of a particular man; an Angel drops on it, from a phial, a tear which the sinner had shed in doing a good action, and his sins are washed out.

Alberic the Monk

Angels mean messengers and ministers. Their function is to execute the plan of Divine providence, even in earthly things.

St. Thomas Aquinas

> *The entire hierarchy of Angels can best be described as an endlessly vast sphere of beings who surround an unknowable center point which is called God.*
>
> Malcolm Godwin

THE MAN IN THE PHOTO

I have two older brothers and they share a room. One day one of my brothers was staying over at a friend's house and for some reason I wanted to sleep in their room with my other brother. Later that night I had a hard time getting to sleep, so I was just lying there. Then, out of nowhere, there was a man sitting on the edge of the bed. I blinked a couple of times to make sure I wasn't seeing things. He didn't say anything; he was just sitting there with his hand on my foot. It felt like he was there forever, but he was only there for a couple of seconds then he just disappeared.

Later that year we went to my grandma's house and I was looking at her photos. When I saw a picture of my grandpa I stood there frozen. My grandpa died four months before I was born, so I had never seen him before. I had never got to experience what it was like to have a grandpa. The man in the photo looked exactly like the man I saw in my brothers' room. To this day, I believe the man I saw was my grandpa and he was there to tell me it's OK and that he is watching over me.

Around our pillows golden ladders rise,
And up and down the skies,
With winged sandals shod,
The angels come, and go, the
messengers of God!

Richard Henry Stoddard

An Angel, then, is an intelligent essence, in perpetual motion, with free will, incorporeal, ministering to God, having obtained by grace an immortal nature; and the Creator alone knew the form and limitation of its nature.

St. John

An angel is a spiritual creature created by God without a body for the service of Christendom and the church.

Martin Luther

A FIGURE IN THE CLOUDS

On a plane from Nevada, after a visit with a friend ended on an empty note, I heard a voice. It said, 'Look out of the window.'

I did so and saw a beautiful figure standing on a flat carpet of clouds. Although he appeared to be made from the clouds, he was not. He stood maybe 40 feet from my window, he was huge (perhaps 8–10 feet tall) and clothed in flowing white. In his hand he held a staff. His wings were folded behind him. He stood watching as I watched him. The image remained unchanged for a minute or so as the plane

passed him. I didn't think of making a sound or asking anyone else to look. I wanted to gaze at him for as long as I could.

It was Easter Day, which was odd to me because I do not celebrate it. Could this have been a trick of the eye and a funny cloud formation? Perhaps – but the voice and what I saw were very real to me. I will never forget it.

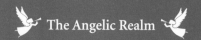

Angels are men of a superior kind; Angels are men in lighter habit clad.

Edward Young

The angels have not bodies naturally united to them. For whatever belongs to any nature as an accident is not found universally in that nature; thus, for instance, to have wings, because it is not of the essence of an animal, does not belong to every animal.

St. Thomas Aquinas

The other things which are lower than the angels are so created that they first receive existence in the knowledge of the rational creature, and then in their own nature.

St. Augustine

'WHERE HAD HE COME FROM?'

When I was about three or four, my mother, older brother and I were in a car accident. I was very young, so I don't remember the details, but I know our car completely flipped over and we landed upside down. The location was a bit secluded, so it would have been a while until someone found us.

I remember being upside down in my car seat, and all of a sudden seeing a man wearing blue jeans and a green

shirt reach into our car and pull my mom out. He then proceeded to pull all of us out of the car. My brother had a bad head injury and was bleeding profusely all over his face. The man took off his shirt and wrapped it round his head.

Someone finally found us and called the emergency services. No one saw the man in green except for me and my family. My mom says she remembers him walking away, but he had no car, no place to go. We were in the mountains.... Where had he come from? We could tell that he wasn't homeless because he was very well-groomed. The fact that we ALL remember this man suggests to me that he was real. To this day, we all believe that he was an angel.

In such green palaces the
    first kings reign'd,
Slept in their shades, and
    angels entertain'd;
With such old counsellors
    they did advise.
And by frequenting sacred
    groves grew wise.

Edmund Waller

The function of the wing is to take what
is heavy and raise it up into the region
above, where the gods dwell; of all things
connected with the body, it has the
greatest affinity with the divine.

Plato

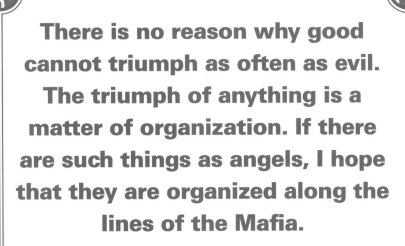

There is no reason why good cannot triumph as often as evil. The triumph of anything is a matter of organization. If there are such things as angels, I hope that they are organized along the lines of the Mafia.

Kurt Vonnegut

ANGELS HOLDING HANDS

When I was five, we went to visit my aunt and uncle. I didn't want to go to bed because they lived in a wooded area and I was afraid of bears and other wild animals. I asked my mom and aunt, 'What will happen if the bears get inside, or if someone sneaks into the house?' My mom responded: 'They can't get inside.' I asked how she knew, and my mom replied, 'Because angels are all around the house.' I looked outside and said, 'Where?' My mom said, 'You can't see them, but they're there.'

When my mom and aunt had left the room, I got up and looked out the window again. It was open, so I stuck my head outside and looked up. There were angels, holding

hands, surrounding the house. In a line spanning as far as I could see – angels! Full-sized, dressed in robes and dresses, suspended in air and seemingly almost stuck to the house. They didn't look at me until I caught the eye of one of them. And he smiled at me.

Since I thought this was what my mom was speaking of, I remember thinking she had lied to me – I could see them! I went to bed and in the morning said: 'I saw those angels last night.' My mom laughed and thought it was cute, but dismissed it as a fib. Years later, I reminded her of it and told her that it was not a fib; I really had seen the angels.

Angels, who are God's messengers, turn themselves into different shapes.

The Zohar

The war broke out in heaven;
Michael and his angels battled
against the dragon. The dragon and
its angels fought back, but they did
not prevail and there was no longer
any place for them in heaven.

Revelation 12:7-9

Where the bright
seraphim in burning row
Their loud uplifted angel
trumpets blow.

John Milton

'WE FLEW HIGH UP INTO THE SKY...'

One afternoon, a few years ago, I was feeling unwell. I went to lie on the bed, but before I fell asleep I was visited by two small angels on either side of me. They picked me up gently and carried me outside. I was excited, but not at all nervous. We flew high up into the sky and they took me to what I believe

were two of my past
lives. I was enchanted.

Afterward they brought
me back to my bed,
kissed me gently and left.
I cried as they flew away.
I begged them to come
back again, but so far
they never have.
I was not dreaming, I
was awake when this
happened and I swear it
really did happen.

Angels (they say) would often not know whether they moved among living or dead. The eternal current sweeps all the ages within it, through both the spheres, forever, and resounds above them in both.

Rainer Maria Rilke

And this is all that is known, and more than all – yet nothing to what the angels know – of the life of a servant of God, who sinned and repented, and did penance and washed out his sins, and became a saint, and reigns with Christ in heaven.

Cardinal Newman

Angels are not merely forms of extraterrestrial intelligence. They are forms of extra-cosmic intelligence.

Mortimer J. Adler

'HER VOICE WAS SO LOVELY...'

Many years ago, my husband was seriously ill. He had been hospitalized many times and we knew that his time was short. I stayed with him day and night in his hospital room.

One night, he was feeling very low and said he felt so alone. I tried to convince him that he was not alone, that God knew where he was and loved him. About three o'clock in the morning, the door to his room opened and in walked what I thought was a nurse. She went to his bedside and called him by his nickname, a name only his close family and friends knew. She told him that God was there with him and loved him dearly. She asked what his favourite song was. He told her 'Amazing Grace'. There, in the early morning hours,

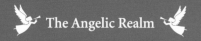

she began to sing. Her voice was so lovely it seemed to fill the room. You could feel the love radiating in the whole room as she sang.

She finished the song, turned and walked quietly out of the room. I wanted to thank her for her kindness and followed her out into the hall. But the hallway was empty and there was no one in sight. I waited for a few minutes, as I thought she had gone into another room. Finally I went to the nurses' station and asked to speak to the nurse who had come into our room. The nurse on duty said that she was the only one assigned to those rooms. Then I knew that God had sent one of his angels to comfort my husband and myself in our time of need.

Some orders are associated with particular divine qualities – Seraphim with Love, Cherubim with Wisdom, Thrones with Judgement.

David Connolly

Now walk the angels on the walls
of heaven,
As sentinels to warn th' immortal souls,
To entertain divine Zenocrate.

Christopher Marlowe

Therefore with Angels
and Archangels, and
with all the company
of heaven, we laud and
magnify thy glorious
Name.

The Book of Common Prayer

DRESSED IN WHITE

Thirty-two years ago I gave birth to my son. At 1.30 a.m., I got ready to feed him. I put the light on over my bed. All of a sudden, the light went out and a lovely lady was at the end of my bed. She looked at me, then at my son who was in a crib at my left-hand side. When I looked back at her she had gone. She was so lovely – blonde,

and dressed in white.
I pressed the bell for the
nurse. When she came, all I
said was that the light had
gone out suddenly. But the
nurse said the light was OK.
I know I did see an angel.

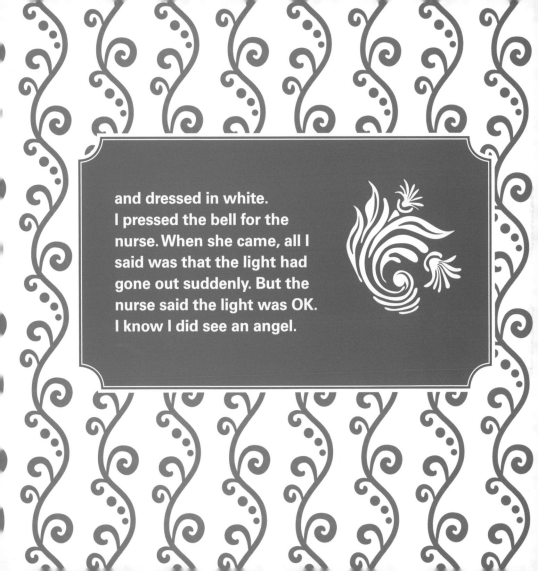

At the round earth's imagined corners, blow
Your trumpets, angels, and arise, arise
From death, you numberless infinities
Of souls, and to your scattered bodies go.

John Donne

*I saw the angels heave up
Sir Lancelot unto heaven,
and the gates of heaven
opened against him.*

Sir Thomas Malory

It must be known that all spirits and angels without exception were once men, for the human race is the seminary of heaven; and that spirits are altogether such as to their affections and inclinations as they had been when they lived as men in the world, for every one's life follows him.

Emanuel Swedenborg

'YOU ARE GOING TO BE OK'

When I was about 19, I started using drugs and really beginning to abuse myself physically and mentally. As time went on, my older sister became concerned and asked me to hang out with her more often, but I always made excuses to avoid her. When I finally agreed to spend the evening with her, she had arranged a blind date for me. The day before I was supposed to meet her, I went to a party that lasted until the following day.

I remember a few things about that night as I lay in my bed: the pain my body was feeling, my sister calling me

to tell me my blind date was waiting, and an image at the foot of my bed as I begged for the pain to go away. It was one of those moments when you cannot tell if it is a dream or if it is real. I was restless. I fell asleep, then woke up to see two people at the foot of my bed. There was a girl on my left side and a boy on my right. They would not look at my face, but just stood there with their heads tilted and said, 'Don't worry, you are going to be OK.'

I woke up the next day to realize a lot about myself and to know those changes could not happen in a day. I am 30 now and drug free. There are many gaps to fill in this story, but I would just like to mention that there are angels out there – whether they be in your dreams or at the foot of your bed.

One more thing: that blind date I was supposed to meet that night? He is the man I am married to now. This is a man who has also brought faith back into my life.

He passed the flaming bounds
of place and time:
The living throne, the sapphire-blaze,
Where angels tremble,
while they gaze,
He saw; but blasted with
excess of light,
Closed his eyes in endless night.

Thomas Gray

Hear all ye angels,
progeny of light,
Thrones, dominations,
princedoms, virtues, powers.

John Milton

PEACHES AND CREAM

It was a Sunday evening and we were returning from church. It had been raining most of the day and the roads were beginning to flood. I had my little granddaughter with me. The road was narrow and I could see water rushing across it. Both my granddaughter and I began to panic. How could we get down the hill with this water rushing over the road?

Suddenly I saw the headlights of a vehicle coming towards us. When it got to us, I rolled down my window and asked the driver if we could get through. He said, 'No, the road is washed away – you must turn round and go another way.' I began to cry and said I couldn't turn my vehicle round and could he please help us. He got out of his truck and got behind the wheel of my car and turned us round. He told us to calm down and to go to the end of the road and turn right. We would be safe then.

I thanked him and started driving down the road. I looked in my mirror and saw his lights following me. Suddenly I forgot which way he had told me to go, so I pulled over to wait for him so that I could follow him. I looked in my rear-view mirror to see his lights coming and there were none. There were no roads to turn off into and no houses – where could he have gone? I decided to drive to the end of the road; when I got there I remembered he said to turn right. We made it back to town safe.

The only thing I remember about him was that he had on a white shirt; I couldn't remember his face. My granddaughter said, 'Grandma, he smelled like peaches and cream.'

I will never forget the angel in white who smelled like peaches and cream that awful night.

God does not deal directly with man: it is by means of spirits that all the intercourse and communication of gods with men, both in waking life and in sleep, is carried on.

Socrates

In the strictest definition, an angel is a superior being living in the spirit world – standing between humans and God.

John Ronner

It is not plainly said whether or when the angels were created; but if mention is made, it is implicit under the name of 'heaven,' when it is said, 'In the beginning God created the heavens and the earth.'

St. Augustine

The earth is to the sun what
man is to the angels.

Victor Hugo

Whether the angels play
only Bach in praising God I
am not quite sure; I am sure,
however, that en famille
they play Mozart.

Karl Barth

Sacred Angels

I saw the tracks of angels in the earth: the beauty of heaven walking by itself on the world.

Petrarch

Thinkest thou that I cannot now pray to my Father, and he shall presently give me more than twelve legions of angels?

Matthew 26:53

If a man perform a religious precept, one angel is assigned to him; if he perform two precepts, two angels are assigned to him; if he perform all the precepts, many angels are assigned to him; as it is said, 'For He shall give His angels charge over you, to keep you in all thy ways.'

Misdrash

A LADY WITH LONG HAIR

When I was seventeen, I had a tumor, which meant I needed spinal cord surgery. As I was waking up from the operation I saw a lady with long hair, all in white, standing next to my bed  and looking down on me with a smile. After a couple of seconds she walked toward the bathroom and disappeared. I wasn't scared; I felt peace in my heart and I knew it was an angel watching over me.

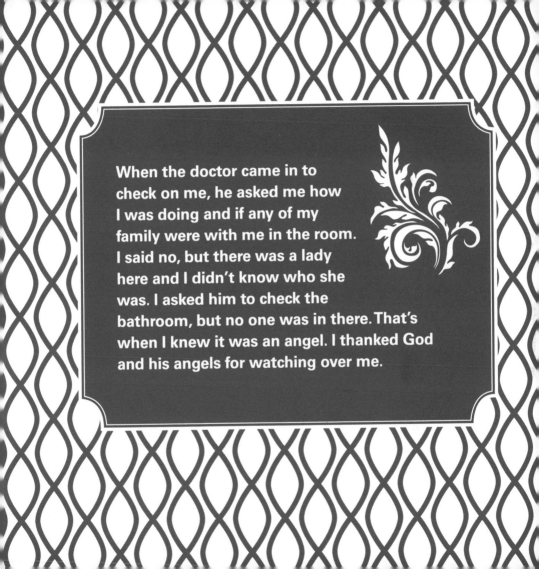

When the doctor came in to check on me, he asked me how I was doing and if any of my family were with me in the room. I said no, but there was a lady here and I didn't know who she was. I asked him to check the bathroom, but no one was in there. That's when I knew it was an angel. I thanked God and his angels for watching over me.

*Every raindrop that
falls is accompanied
by an angel, for
every raindrop is a
manifestation of
a being.*

The Koran

How do the angels get to sleep
when the devil leaves the porch light on?

Tom Waits

*Mounted on a mighty angel he flew, soaring on
the wings of the wind.*

Psalm 18:10

'I AM AN ANGEL SENT FROM GOD...'

I am 25 years old. A few years ago I had a pretty bad drug problem. It got so bad that one night I was overdosing. I was rushed to the emergency room. The doctors and nurses were trying to hold me down so they could put a shot into my chest (they told me later it was to slow my heart rate down). Despite their efforts I was frantic and would not stay still long enough to let them put a shot in my chest.

As I was screaming, shaking and struggling, a lady walked in the room. She was blonde and very pure looking. I remember the doctors and nurses didn't even look at her or acknowledge she was in the room. She said to me, 'I am an angel sent from God to save you. I need

you to calm down so the doctors can put the medicine in your body.' Her voice was so soothing, that as soon as she spoke my body completely relaxed and was at peace. Despite the chaos in the room, she was smiling and very calm and peaceful…as if it was almost humorous that people would be worried about anything.

After coming round 17 hours later I asked the nurse who was in the room that night about the blonde lady who had calmed me down by telling me she was an angel. I said I wanted to thank her. The nurse told me that she had been the only woman in the room that night.

It was an angel and she even told me so!

It must be affirmed that angels and everything existing, except God, were made by God.

St. Thomas Aquinas

The man form is higher than the angel form; of all forms it is the highest. Man is the highest being in creation, because he aspires to freedom.

Paramahansa Yogananda

Behold I say unto you, Nay; for it is by faith that miracles are wrought; and it is by faith that angels appear and minister unto men; wherefore, if these things have ceased, woe be unto the children of men, for it is because of unbelief.

Moroni 6:36-37

'THREE ANGELS STOOD BY MY BED…'

When my daughter was two years old she was diagnosed with cancer. Her temperature was sky high and she was flown by helicopter to a children's hospital some 200 miles away.

When I arrived in her room, the priest was giving her last rites. I immediately left the room so that she would not see me break down.

I returned shortly afterward to find her sleeping soundly. Throughout the night, the nurses were in and out of the room to change her I.V. and check her vitals.

The next morning my daughter informed me that the angels had been in to see her (I assumed she meant the nurses.) My daughter said, 'Three angels stood by my bed, one touched my hand and with her mind told me I was going to be OK. They were beautiful, they wore long white dresses and were shiny.'

There is no doubt in my mind, or within the minds of the rest of our family, that our daughter was visited by angels who were watching over her while she fought a battle that many others have lost. God sent his angels to let us know we were not alone in our fear and pain.

 Sacred Angels

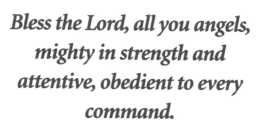

Bless the Lord, all you angels, mighty in strength and attentive, obedient to every command.

Psalm 103.20

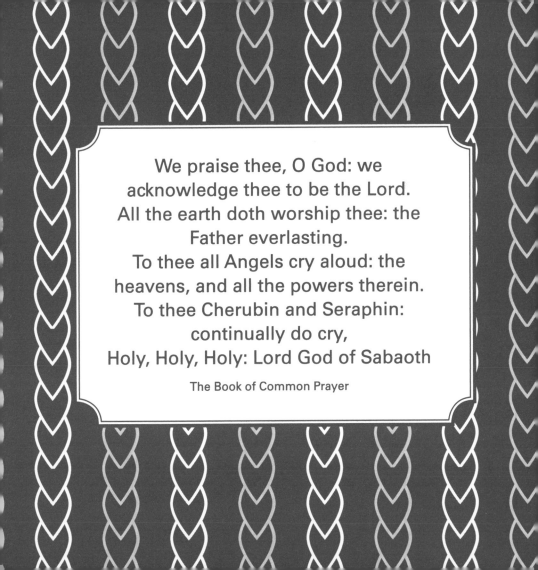

We praise thee, O God: we acknowledge thee to be the Lord. All the earth doth worship thee: the Father everlasting. To thee all Angels cry aloud: the heavens, and all the powers therein. To thee Cherubin and Seraphin: continually do cry, Holy, Holy, Holy: Lord God of Sabaoth

The Book of Common Prayer

'MY HUSBAND HAD DIED...'

My husband and I were heading home from the doctor's when he started complaining about fire in his chest, then started gurgling and passed out. I pulled over to check his pulse and found he didn't have one. I said, 'God help me! What do I do?' I heard a voice in the back seat say, 'Hit him in the chest.' I raised my fist to hit him and then I said, 'Where?' I felt someone grab my arm, swing it

and hit my husband three times. He came round. Then I looked in the back seat and there was no one there. I was a block from home, so called a friend and he phoned the emergency room and they met me. They told me my husband had had a heart attack; hitting him in the chest had started his heart beating again. God had sent an angel to save my husband in the nick of time.

May Michael be at my right hand and
Gabriel at my left, before me Uriel and
Raphael behind, and above my head
the divine presence of God.

Jewish prayer

To worship at the feet of the angels, when
all men worship only fame and riches, is
not easy. But the most difficult of all is to
think the thoughts of the angels, to speak
the words of the angels, and to do as the
angels do.

Gospel of the Essenes

*For thou hast made him a
little lower than the angels,
and hast crowned him
with glory and honour.*

Psalm 8:5

'THEY HAD THIS GLOW ABOUT THEM...'

A couple of years ago, my parents and I had been shopping. We decided to take the back roads and go the long way home to skip the highways. We heard a big pop and dad got out of the car and saw we had a flat. We were in the middle of nowhere, with no one to be seen, miles from the nearest home or stores. We had no extra tire and it was pitch black outside.

After a few minutes, two young men stopped their car and asked if we needed help. They were very kind and

gentle; almost non-human. They had this glow about them. They had an extra tire the exact size we needed and they fixed our flat like they had done it a million times before. We told them thank you, and asked if there was anything we could do for them. They told us that we all get in trouble sometimes and there was no need to thank them. They gave my dad a pat on the back and gave me and mom a hug and said, 'God bless you, God is with you', then disappeared into thin air. We looked everywhere for them. I don't know what happened that night, but I believe those men were angels and they were watching over us. All I can say is it was a miracle.

*I believe in angels because the
Bible says there are angels;
and I believe the Bible to be
the true Word of God.*

Billy Graham

Come and see. When
the sun sets, the
cherubim...beat their
wings above and
stretch them out, and
the melodious sound of
their wings is heard in
the realms above.

The Zohar

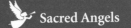

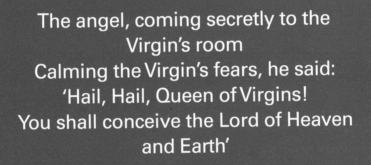

The angel, coming secretly to the
Virgin's room
Calming the Virgin's fears, he said:
'Hail, Hail, Queen of Virgins!
You shall conceive the Lord of Heaven
and Earth'

Anonymous, medieval carol

ANSWER TO A PRAYER

I lost my job and was in dire straits thinking of what to do and where to turn. I prayed to God all day to send me a sign that it would be OK. A man came to my door one afternoon. He was an old man, but had the youngest, most beautiful eyes I have ever seen. The only way I can

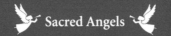

describe them is 'pure'. He was selling Archangel Michael cards with a medal and a prayer, a prayer that said all I needed to hear. I don't know who this man was, but whoever he was I thank God and the angels for letting me know that they are here and with me no matter what happens to me.

FELLOW PASSENGER

I live in Toronto, Canada.
I had taken the streetcar
down town because I was
going for a job interview. As
I approached my destination,
it began to snow so heavily
I couldn't see. Just before
getting to my stop, I got up
and went to the door. I tried
to look for traffic, but couldn't
see anything. Beside me on
the stairs was a man who I
assumed would be getting off
at the same stop.

The doors opened at my
stop and I was about to get

off when I noticed that the man made no move. I was distracted by this. At that moment, a tractor trailer whizzed by the streetcar. I thought, 'Oh my gosh – I could have been killed!'

I turned to thank the man, but he had vanished. I asked others on the bus if they had seen the man, but they said there was nobody there. I am convinced that God sent an angel. If he had not been there, I would have stepped off and been killed instantly.

For He shall give his angels charge over thee,
to keep thee in all thy ways.

Psalm 91:11

Now long ago I sat and listened to the angels at this hour, and marvelled how they cried out; their cry was like the noise of a mighty wheel, and they cried out like the waves of the sea with the voice of praise to God.

The Testament of Adam

Every blade of grass has an angel that bends over it and whispers, 'grow! grow!'

The Talmud

ANGELIC BABYSITTER

When I was 19 years old I was in love with a girl named Mindy. I went to see her one night, and the most incredible thing happened.

When I pulled up at her house, I saw the front door was open. Mindy's little brothers and sisters were sitting on the stairs and there was a lady in a white robe standing directly behind them. I thought the lady was their mom, so I waved and smiled at her and said 'Hi, is Mindy here?' She just looked at me, then turned her head and walked down the hall. That was kind of rude, I thought, but maybe she was embarrassed because she had just gotten out of the tub and was wearing a robe.

I walked up to the kids and said, 'Hey, is Mindy here?' They said, 'No, she's not.' Then I said, 'Would you go get your mom then?' They said, 'She's not here. If you don't believe us, come in.' I walked up the stairs and down

the hall where the woman had been three minutes before. There were two bedrooms and I walked into both of them. I opened the closet doors and looked under the beds. Then I walked up to the windows to check she hadn't jumped out. She had totally vanished.

The next morning, Mindy and her mom came to my house. Mindy's mom pulled out a picture and said, 'Is this the lady you saw?' I said 'Yes, but I thought it was you!' She replied, 'This is my mother, but she has been dead for ten years!' She said that last night she and her husband had prayed that their kids would be protected until they got home.

Whenever you can, always pray that your children will be protected, because sometimes they literally are!

While shepherds watched
their flocks by night,
All seated on the ground,
The angel of the Lord
came down,
And glory shone around.

Nahum Tate

Those who have said, 'Our Lord is God', then have gone straight, upon them the angels descend, saying, 'Fear not, neither sorrow; rejoice in Paradise that you were promised. We are your friends in the present life and in the world to come; therein you shall have all that your souls desire...'

The Koran

'THEY PULLED MY DAD FROM THE WRECKAGE...'

My dad is a truck driver. One evening in 1995 he was driving down a road in the middle of the countryside. Another truck was driving toward him. It slammed into my dad's driver side door, flipping his truck over. The impact knocked my dad out and a fire started in his cab.

Just then, a car drove up and two men got out and ran to the truck. They pulled my dad from the wreckage and carried him across the road into a small ravine. Soon after, the truck exploded into flames.

The driver who had hit my dad's truck called the

police. My dad was taken to hospital where he suffered slight burns, loss of hearing and some scrapes and bruises. But nothing was broken and no internal organs were damaged. When the police checked their report for the names of the two men, they saw they had written 'Gabriel' and 'Michael'. There were no last names on the paper. When my parents tried to contact these men, they couldn't find them anywhere. The police were baffled because they recall that the men had given their last names and addresses.

God had sent two of his angels down to save my father.

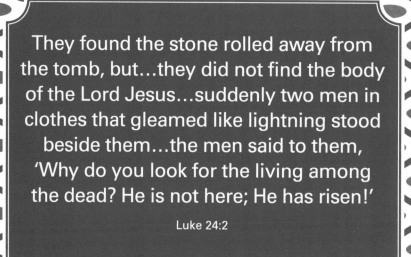

They found the stone rolled away from the tomb, but…they did not find the body of the Lord Jesus…suddenly two men in clothes that gleamed like lightning stood beside them…the men said to them, 'Why do you look for the living among the dead? He is not here; He has risen!'

Luke 24:2

Behold, I send an Angel before thee, to keep thee in the way, and to bring thee into the place which I have prepared.

Exodus 23:20

MY OWN PERSONAL ANGEL

I've been in two major car accidents that I probably should not have lived through, but I am still here, by the grace of God – and, I think, my grandma. She died in 1979, before I was born. Before she died she gave my mother a baby bible, just like she had given my two older sisters bibles when they were babies. Although my mother was not planning on having more children, my grandma insisted she have the bible. Three years later, I accidentally came along.

About a year ago, I was heading home in my car when my four-year-old son, who was sitting in the back

seat, suddenly said, 'Hi, Grandma.' I asked him who he was talking to, and he said, 'Grandma'. Thinking he was talking about my other grandma, who's still living, I responded, 'Honey, Grandma's at home'. He said, 'No, Mommy, Grandma – right there!' I glanced over my shoulder quickly at him and he was pointing at the empty passenger seat as he said it.

Even though my grandma died before I was born, I'm so lucky to have her as my own personal angel in the passenger seat.

It came upon the midnight clear,
That glorious song of old,
From Angels bending near the earth
To touch their harps of gold;
'Peace on the earth, good will to man
From Heaven's all gracious King.'
The world in solemn stillness lay
To hear the angels sing.

Edmund Hamilton Sears

He rained down manna also upon them for to eat: and gave them food from heaven. So man did eat angels' food: for he sent them meat enough.

Psalm 78: 25

'SOMEONE PICKED UP THE PHONE...'

My mother is 82 and has a rare form of cancer and several other illnesses. She is the most loving, generous woman I know, but has had such an unhappy life, mentally and physically. She stays with me five days a week and goes to her apartment at weekends.

Last Saturday she mentioned she was feeling dizzy and a bit unwell. This happens often, so I told her to rest and said I would phone her later.

I was walking my dog at a park near her apartment when I called her on my cell phone. Her phone rang at least 25 times. I knew she was there and became worried when she didn't answer. I called again and, after about 13 rings, someone picked up the phone. Very faintly in the background I could hear her calling my name. I asked if she was hurt.

I could hear her saying that she had fallen and was on the kitchen floor. I told her I would be right there. But how had she answered the phone?

When I got to her apartment I found my mom on the floor and both phones still on the hook. She could not have moved to answer them! She lives alone and no one else was there. Whoever picked up the phone saved my mom's life. I thank God and my mom's guardian angels for allowing my call to get through to her. I believe in miracles, but I'm still numb from this experience.

And suddenly there was with the angel a multitude of the heavenly host praising God and saying, 'Glory to God in the highest, and on earth peace, good will toward men!'

Luke 2:13

Angels are our true and trusty servants, performing offices and works that one poor miserable mendicant would be ashamed to do for another.

Martin Luther

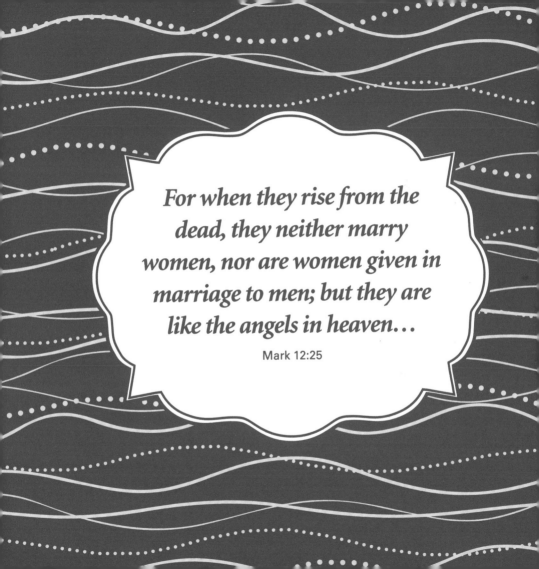

For when they rise from the dead, they neither marry women, nor are women given in marriage to men; but they are like the angels in heaven…

Mark 12:25

ANGELIC OPERATION

My grandfather, who lives in Durban, South Africa, had the following vision while I was undergoing surgery in the United States:

'I am writing this letter to tell you what I saw when you underwent the surgery. I saw three angels around you. Two of them, one on your left and one on your right, were stroking your arms and talking to you, telling you not to be afraid and that the Lord will hear you. They were

dressed in light peach-coloured garments, they were laughing and talking to you all the time. The third angel stood at the head of the bed, directing and telling the surgeon what to do and how to do it. Praise the Lord! A fourth angel was outside the operating room, comforting your mom and dad with its wings spread over them, telling them not to fear as God is in control. Praise God for His healing power!'

*They take different forms at the bidding
of their Master, God, and thus reveal
themselves to men and unveil the Divine
mysteries to them.*

St. John

Above all, angels are
participants with us in the
glory of creation. They sing
the wonders of God
and the cosmos. Their song is
ours to sing too.

Rosemary Ellen Guiley

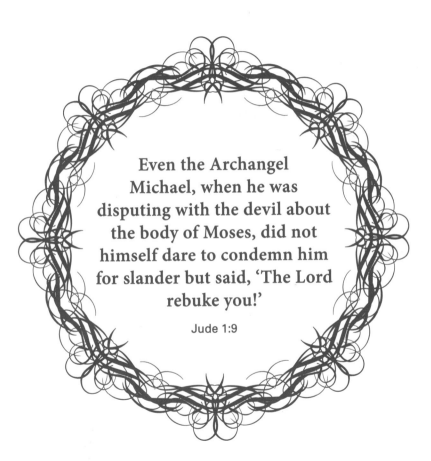

Even the Archangel
Michael, when he was
disputing with the devil about
the body of Moses, did not
himself dare to condemn him
for slander but said, 'The Lord
rebuke you!'

Jude 1:9

AN ANGEL HUGGED ME

My mom died of cancer when I was nine years old. I had so many things on my mind…I cried and cried about my problems just about every night.

Years later, just before my graduation, I had a dream. In my dream I was sitting in the living room doing my homework. I had this weird feeling that someone was staring at me. When I looked up, I saw my mom standing there. I was lost for words. She came to me, grabbed me by the hand and took me outside on the porch. She looked at me, gave me a little smile and hugged me for about two long minutes. She didn't say a word to me,

but gave me that look that said, 'Don't worry about anything, it's going to be all right.' I just looked at her and she looked so good, like she did before she was diagnosed with cancer.

She let me go, kissed my forehead, and walked away. I screamed after her, 'Where are you going? Will I ever see you again?' She said nothing, but turned around and smiled; there were wings on her back, and it was all white outside. She was my angel. She came to tell me not to worry so much. And, sure enough, I graduated, and got a few scholarships I never thought I would get.

Very truly I tell you, you will see heaven open, and the angels of God ascending and descending on the Son of Man.

John 1:50

I saw Gabriel, like a maiden or like the moon amongst the stars. His hair was like a woman's, falling in long tresses... He is the most beautiful of Angels.

Ruzbehan Baqli

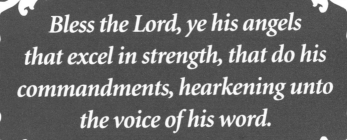

Bless the Lord, ye his angels that excel in strength, that do his commandments, hearkening unto the voice of his word.

Psalm 103:20

A GARMENT MADE OF LIGHT

I had been going through stress for several years and situations around me were getting worse – I was at the edge of losing my sanity. I began crying, it became almost uncontrollable. The pain I was feeling was tremendous, and the thoughts that raced through my mind were insane. I curled myself into a knot and yelled out to God to help me.

All of a sudden, a being was standing before me. He glowed so magnificently and his beauty was

gloriously perfect. He stood about six feet tall and wore a long white garment made of light. His face and hair were a different shade of light, but all of him glowed bright as the sun. He raised his hand toward me with his palm facing me. He reached out to me until his palm touched my forehead. As he touched me, the pressure of my pain and stress began to subside, all the way down my body, until it was no more. The angel had disappeared with the same swiftness he had appeared.

And there appeared to him an angel from heaven, to strengthen him. And he was in fear, and prayed earnestly; and his sweat became like drops of blood.

Luke 22:43

September 29 is the feast day for the three Angels mentioned by name in the Bible – Michael, Gabriel, and Raphael.

John Ronner

And I saw another Angel fly in the midst of heaven, having the everlasting gospel to preach unto them that dwell on the earth, and to every nation, and kindred, and tongue, and people.

Revelation 14:6

The cherubim shall spread out their wings above, overshadowing the mercy seat with their wings, their faces one to another; toward the mercy seat shall the faces of the cherubim be.

Exodus 25:20

Sacred Angels

O come, all ye faithful,
Joyful and triumphant,
O come ye, O come ye to Bethlehem;
Come and behold him,
Born the King of angels.

A carol from Murray's Hymnal

Neither can they die any more: for they are equal unto the angels.

Luke 20:36

A CALM PRESENCE

Twelve years ago, I had a small apartment and lived alone. One night I had a sudden feeling of dread as I was lying in bed. A dark figure approached and lay down on top of me. I could not breathe or move. I was horrified. This thing looked three-dimensional, but was made of shadow. It was terrifying. I prayed very hard for it to go away.

Suddenly, something came and sat on my bed. I could not see a figure, but could see the indentation of where it was sitting and

actually felt the bed move. A feeling of calm and serenity came over me. All I felt was love, and that everything was going to be OK.
I fell into a deep sleep and woke up the next morning still feeling like there was a calm presence in the room.

It took me almost a year to tell my boyfriend, now my husband, about the incident. I thought he would think I was crazy. But I think it was an angel sent by God to protect me from this evil entity.

O sovereign angel,
Wide winged stranger
above a forgetful earth,
Care for me, care for me,
Keep me unaware of danger

Edna St. Vincent Millay

 Sacred Angels

And lo, the angel of the Lord came
upon them, and the glory of the
Lord shone round about them, and
they were sore afraid. And the
angel said unto them, 'Fear not,
for behold, I bring you good
tidings of great joy, which
shall be to all people. For
unto you is born this day in
the City of David a Saviour,
who is Christ the Lord.'

Luke 2:9

There are many things which please the Angels, and which it delights them to see in us, like sobriety, chastity, voluntary poverty, repeated signs of desire for Heaven, prayers accompanied with tears and with the heart truly directed to God.

St. Bernard

He who has fed a stranger may have fed an Angel.

The Talmud

Guardian Angels

We cannot pass our
guardian angel's bounds,
Resigned or sullen, he will hear our sighs.

John Keble

Who are these angels? They are his guardians
from the harmful spirits; as it is said,
'A thousand shall fall at your side and ten
thousand at your right hand.'

The Midrash

Sleep, my child, and peace attend thee
All through the night.
Guardian angels God will send thee,
All through the night.

Sir Harold Boulton

A COMFORTING VOICE

Driving home one evening, I noticed a vehicle coming toward me at high speed.
I changed lanes to avoid it.
But the vehicle changed lanes with me, and headed straight at me.
I gripped the steering wheel, stepped on the brake, and shut my eyes. As the vehicle hit me head-on at 85 mph, I felt something holding me, like a great big hug. Then everything went black.

I woke up lying halfway out of my vehicle, on the other side of the highway. There was someone sitting with me, shielding the rain

from me and assuring me that help would soon come. I passed out again.

When I woke up, there were multiple firefighters, medics and police officers trying to free me from the car. They rushed me to hospital, where I found that my hips and pelvis had been crushed and I was suffering a hematoma (bleed) on the left side of my brain. I found out that the young man driving the other vehicle had died immediately.

After recovering from surgery, I wanted to thank the person who had stayed by my side until rescue arrived, but discovered that no one had been there when a police officer found us. I remember the comforting voice as if it were yesterday, but can't describe a look or even say if it was male or female.

We're all kissed by angels, but some of us never think to pucker.

Amethyst Snow-Rivers

The servants of Christ are protected by invisible, rather than visible, beings. But if these guard you, they do so because they have been summoned by your prayer.

St. Ambrose

*If you wish success in life, make
perseverance your bosom friend,
experience your wise counsellor, caution
your elder brother, and hope your
guardian angel.*

Joseph Addison

A HELPING HAND

I was moving a couch into my apartment from my truck. I had it almost inside, but was completely exhausted and drained. A man showed up out of the blue and offered to help me. I lived in a not so good area at the time, so everything in me said to tell him no, but I said 'Sure' because I was so exhausted. He pushed it into my apartment and when I turned round to thank him, he was gone. I went out to the street and tried to find him, but it was like he vanished!

It is at the hour of death that the good angel shows the greatest zeal in protecting and defending the soul committed to his care, invoking often the assistance of other angels against the wiles and fury of Satan.

Pascal Parente

 **Guardian Angels**

For God commands the angels to guard you in all your ways.

Psalms 91:11

Angels are inseparable friends, who bring strength and consolation to those who include them in their lives. In truth, angels are our best friends.

Janice T. Connell

If we truly love our Guardian Angel, we cannot fail to have boundless confidence in his powerful intercession with God and firm faith in his willingness to help us.

St. Bernard of Clairveaux

LUCKY ESCAPE

My aunt was in the car with my grandmother at a stop
light for about five minutes. Finally, the light turned green
and my grandmother, who was driving, tried moving the
gear selector back into drive mode, but it was stuck. She
became angry and tried harder, but it wouldn't budge.
She looked up to see a drunk driver racing through a
red light; he would have crashed into her had she been
moving forward. We believe that her guardian angel had
been holding her back.

Everything we call a trial, a sorrow, or a duty;
Believe me, that Angel's hand is there.

Fra Giovanni

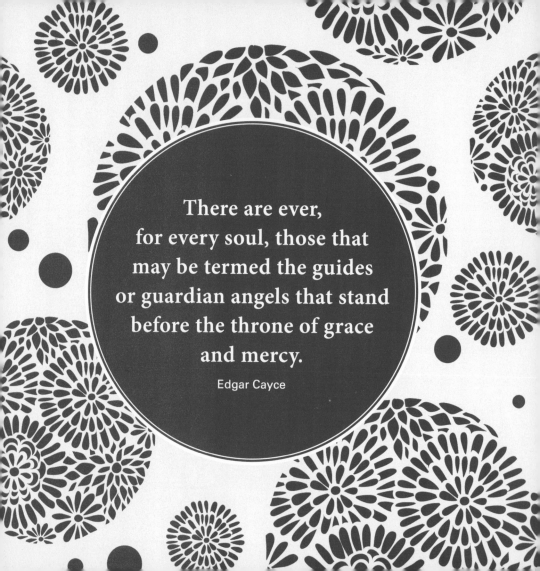

There are ever,
for every soul, those that
may be termed the guides
or guardian angels that stand
before the throne of grace
and mercy.

Edgar Cayce

For a good angel will go with him, his journey will be successful, and he will come home safe and sound.

Tobit 5:21

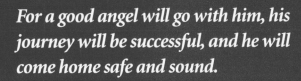

In the Roman Catholic Church calendar, October 2 is the day for honoring guardian angels.

John Ronner

AQUATIC ANGEL

In 2014, an extraordinary photograph posted online by the Tampa police department caught the moment a lost dog was rescued from a river – with the aid of a most unlikely angel. A giant manatee can clearly be seen waiting underwater to protect the dog from the numerous alligators in the area. It is believed the manatee was attracted by the dog's whimpering, and it remained with the animal until rescuers arrived. Manatees are vegetarian, so this one would not have been interested in the dog as prey. The dog was soon

reunited with his owner. He had suffered bug bites and bloody paws, but was otherwise fine.

Department spokeswoman Andrea Davis said: 'This is the kind of image that gives people hope and reminds them there is kindness out there. It's something that can easily make you smile. I think we want to believe that the manatee was the guardian angel. I'm not sure that we'll ever know, but you hear so many bad things, it's good to see an image like this.'

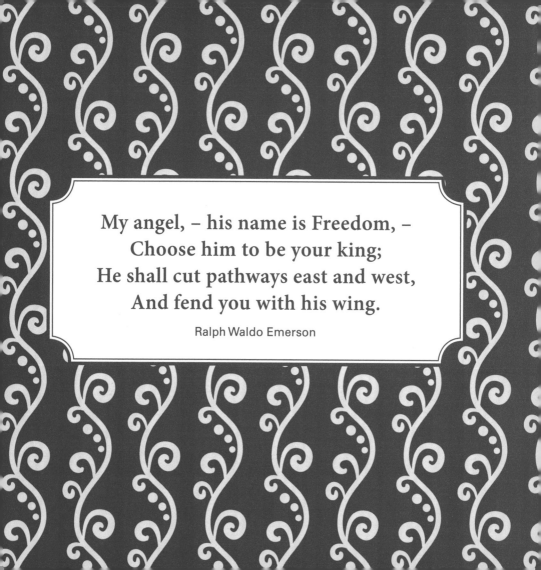

My angel, – his name is Freedom, –
Choose him to be your king;
He shall cut pathways east and west,
And fend you with his wing.

Ralph Waldo Emerson

Angels and ministers of grace defend us.

William Shakespeare

God assures us that his angels are always nearby, ready to help. This is what matters.

Timothy Jones

WHITE FEATHERS

British television presenter Gloria Hunniford believes she receives messages from her daughter Caron, who died from breast cancer at the age of 41. She told reporters: 'I am convinced that Caron has been my guardian angel. People may think I am deluded, but I know she is there for me, protecting and comforting me whenever I need her most.

Like many people, I was once sceptical about the existence of angels. But, as time has passed, I have become completely convinced Caron is an angel whose primary task is to watch out for me. How else to explain

some of the extraordinary things that have happened since her death?'

Gloria describes how Caron leaves white feathers for her as a sign that she is watching over her. She has collected hundreds of them, which she keeps in jars around her house. Before she died, Caron told Gloria: 'Remember, Mum. If an isolated white feather appears out of nowhere, it's a sign that your guardian angel is watching over you.' Gloria says, 'I am convinced she is always close to me, her pockets filled with feathers to drop at my feet when I need her comforting presence most.'

Guardian Angels

My god has sent his angel and
hath shut the lions' mouths,
and they have not hurt me.

Daniel 6:22

Angels need an assumed body, not for themselves, but on our account; that by conversing familiarly with men they may give evidence of that intellectual companionship which men expect to have with them in the life to come.

St. Thomas Aquinas

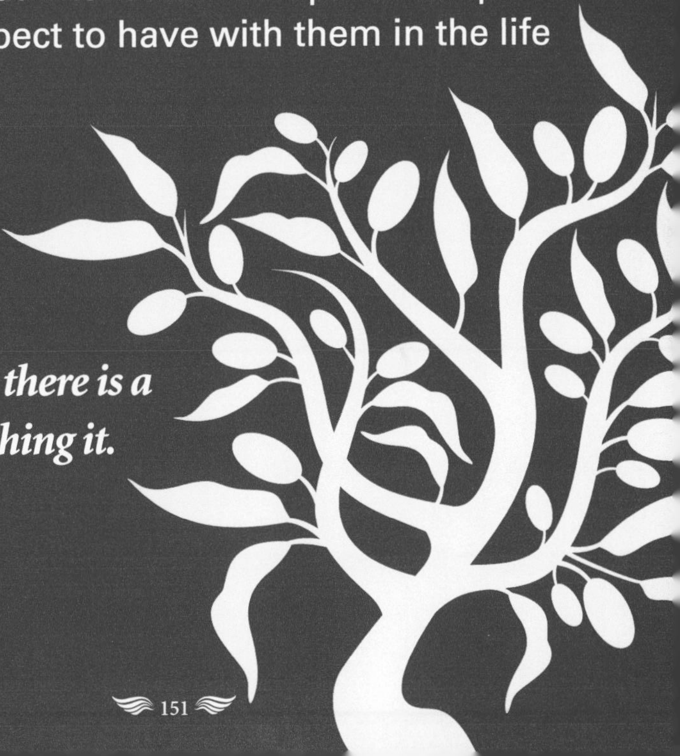

For every soul, there is a guardian watching it.

The Koran

'I WOKE UP SCREAMING...'

My son and I were in the car about two blocks from our destination when I fell asleep – only for seconds – while driving. I woke up screaming, with a tree within a foot of the front of my car! I later learned that a lone driver had overtaken my vehicle and noticed that it disappeared from sight in his rear-view mirror. He had notified the police.

My son and I (and the car) suffered absolutely no harm whatsoever! As the car was being backed out of the area, the police found that I had run over a narrow tree which had given way completely because the ground was so wet from previous rain. I had also missed a light-post and a road sign. One of the officers asked me where I went to church!

Do guardian angels exist? Absolutely!

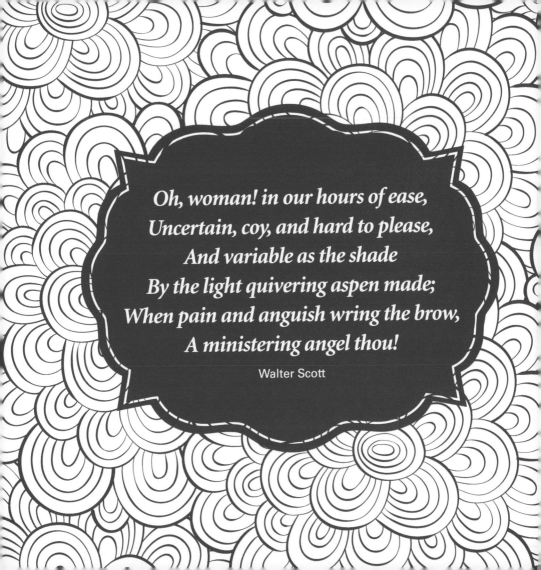

Oh, woman! in our hours of ease,
Uncertain, coy, and hard to please,
And variable as the shade
By the light quivering aspen made;
When pain and anguish wring the brow,
A ministering angel thou!

Walter Scott

The angel of the Lord encampeth round about them that fear Him, and delivereth them.

Psalm 34:7

We not only live among men, but there are airy hosts, blessed spectators, sympathetic lookers-on, that see and know and appreciate our thoughts and feelings and acts.

Henry Ward Beecher

Let your holy Angel have charge concerning us, that the wicked one have no power over us.

Martin Luther

'SOMEONE WAS PUSHING ME OUT OF BED...'

My wife's nephew, Roger, came to stay with us for the night. He was only around three or four at the time. Roger really liked to come visit and play with our younger son, who was a few years older than him.

In the middle of the night, I felt someone trying to push me out of bed. I heard a voice saying, 'Look for Roger, look for Roger', so I jumped out of bed and went to my son's room. Roger was nowhere to be seen. I woke my wife and she went and looked in our son's room again.

I went down to the living room to find the front door wide open. As I walked through it, I looked to my left and saw Roger walking down the sidewalk, about to turn the corner. I yelled out to my wife, who ran after him and brought him home. I really don't know why he walked out of the apartment that day – I guess he was sleep-walking.

This experience has made me a more spiritual person. I truly believe a guardian angel was sent to look after Roger that night.

KNOCK THREE TIMES

I was ill with a bad cold. My mom told me that if I needed her in the night I should knock three times real hard on the wall (we lived in a trailer) and the dogs would bark and wake her up.

At around 2 a.m., I woke feeling horrible. I was coughing and knew I had a fever. I didn't want to wake my mom, so I grabbed a pillow and a blanket and went into her room. I lay down on the floor at the end of her bed.

As the night went on, I found it harder and harder to muffle the sound of my coughs. Eventually I started silently praying to God to please help me. A little while later, I heard my mom get up. She pressed her hand to

my forehead and put a thermometer in my mouth. The first thing she said was, 'Thank goodness you knocked!' She told me my temperature was around 102.

'But mom, I didn't knock. I didn't want to wake you up', I said. My mom was quiet for a little bit. Then she said, 'Baby, your guardian angel woke me up. I heard three loud knocks. You didn't hear them?'

I shook my head. 'God answered my prayer then', I told her. That was when I realized God really does listen, and really does love me.

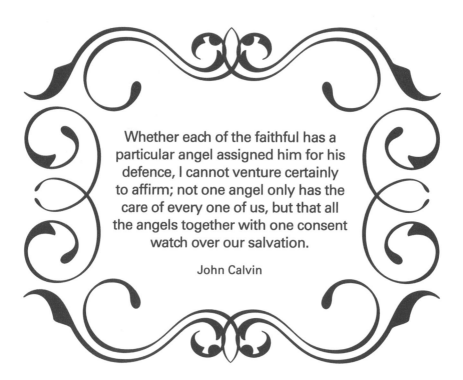

Whether each of the faithful has a particular angel assigned him for his defence, I cannot venture certainly to affirm; not one angel only has the care of every one of us, but that all the angels together with one consent watch over our salvation.

John Calvin

I tell them all of my troubles when they seem too much to bear,
And I put my faith and confidence in their almighty care.

Martina Tarandek

Guardian Angels

If I told you that hundreds of angels with wings dipped in lustrous white pearls, several skies away, line up in our clear-blue moonlit night sky just to admire the glistening shimmer of your soul, would you believe me?

Because they do.

Mustafa Tattan

Guardian Angels

There's a perfect form of tragedy
When two stars cross up above
And an angel and a devil
Find themselves in love

Sydney Esther Thier

For every man that Bolingbroke hath pressed
To lift shrewd steel against our golden crown,
God for his Richard hath in heavenly pay
A glorious angel; then, if angels fight,
Weak men must fall, for heaven still guards the right.

William Shakespeare

Guardian angels are perhaps the most popular kind, probably because we all know how fragile life can be. We desperately need protection from unexpected circumstances and unseen dangers. Just the thought of good angels hovering around us gives people a feeling of safety!

Gary Kinnaman

ANGELIC HANDS

When I was about nine years old my mother took me down to a creek near our house so I could cool off and have fun on a very hot summer's day. I didn't know how to swim, but I enjoyed playing in the water.

I was standing on a big rock when my feet slipped and I fell in the water and went under. Every time I came up I tried to yell for help but couldn't get the word out before I went under again. I know I went under the water three times, but it could have been four.

All of a sudden I felt hands under my arms. It was a physical feeling as though a person was helping me. When I had my feet solidly back on the rock, the hands disappeared. I turned round to say 'thank you', but there was no one there. The closest people were sitting on the bank on the other side of the creek, about two hundred feet away. And I turned round just a few seconds after the hands had gone.

There is no doubt in my mind that an angel saved me that day from drowning.

Guardian Angels

The magnitude of
life is overwhelming.
Angels are here to
help us take it peace
by peace.

Levende Waters

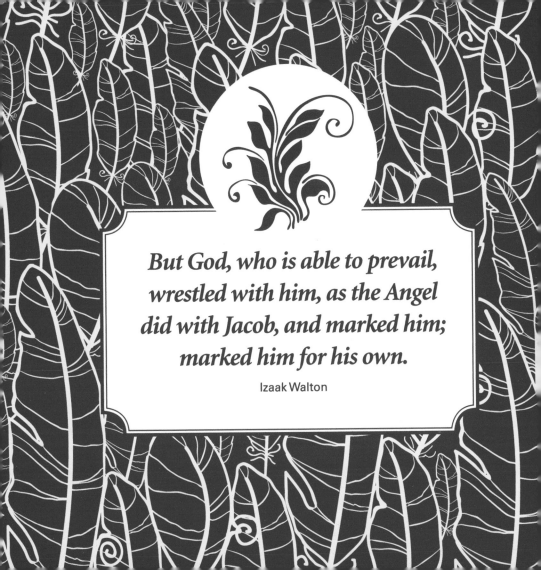

But God, who is able to prevail, wrestled with him, as the Angel did with Jacob, and marked him; marked him for his own.

Izaak Walton

'I HAVE YOU...'

When my sister, an airline stewardess, came home for the holidays, she invited me to go with her to Hawaii. This was a dream for me: I had never been to the ocean before. But one day while I was alone, I swam out too far and found myself across the reef. I was in the current heading away from land, and in high swells rather than the protected bay. When my energy gave out, I slowly sank in the water. I remember looking up at the surface of the ocean from under, maybe, three feet of water and feeling so tranquil.

Then a voice said 'I have you' and a strong arm wrapped itself round my neck, and almost instantly I was in

shallow water near the beach. When I turned to thank the person who had saved me, no one was there.

I was a changed person after that encounter, as many friends and family observed. I went on to finish college and I have had a long and gratifying career as an engineer, which has taken me all over the globe.

For all of you who read this story: never doubt the existence of God, Jesus, heaven and angels. Never forget who you are, where you came from and what you are here for.

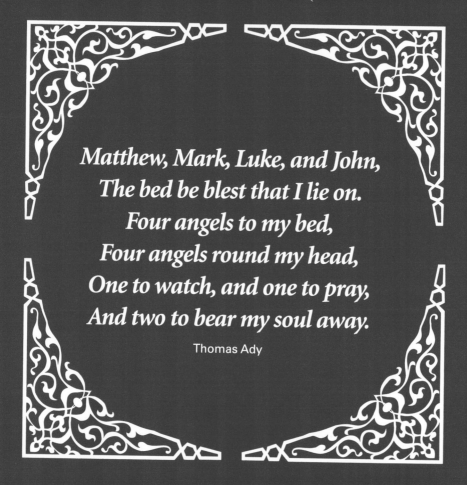

Matthew, Mark, Luke, and John,
The bed be blest that I lie on.
Four angels to my bed,
Four angels round my head,
One to watch, and one to pray,
And two to bear my soul away.

Thomas Ady

Angels help us remember, when the urgencies screaming for attention make us forget, when we feel so estranged by stress or worldliness that we miss the many-splendoured things.

Timothy Jones

Your two guardian angels are always with you. The other angels come and go as we need them.

Doreen Virtue

How wonderful it must be, to speak the language of Angels, with no words for hate and a million words for love!

Eileen Elias Freeman

Death makes angels of us all and gives us wings where we had shoulders smooth as ravens' claws.

Jim Morrison

Angels help you laugh at life, even when you don't think it's funny.

Karen Goldman

We shall find peace. We shall hear the angels, we shall see the sky sparkling with diamonds.

Anton Chekhov

When we are
overcome by some
evil will, should we not
tremble before
the presence of the
choirs of angels that
surround us?

St. Hilary

The angels as the guardians of men are set over men as instructors and monitors…. He is to follow the lead of the angels, and consequently some reverence is already implied in the very relationship that exists between man and angel.

Tertullian

'Christian! seek not yet repose,'
Hear thy guardian angel say;
Thou art in the midst of foes –
'Watch and pray.'

Charlotte Elliott

GUARDIAN GRANDMA

Jon reported that the face of his deceased grandmother was visible in a scan of his baby daughter. He and his wife didn't notice the face at first, but his mother drew their attention to it. Their daughter Madison is now six and also claims to have seen her 'Great Nan Kath' in the front room of her grandparents' house. Jon said: 'I didn't know what to think at first. It was just strange – but it wasn't a worried feeling. We like to think it's Madison's guardian angel, watching over her.'

A BIG PUSH

I had to catch a bus to get to a job. When the bus pulled over at a stop to let me get off, my gloves flew off into the road. Without thinking, I dove to get them – right into the path of the oncoming traffic.

Just as I was about to go forward, a big push sent me backward onto my butt. The next thing I knew, a car barely missed me. I know that if I had not been given that shove, I would be dead. There was no one at the bus stop with me, and the bus had left. An angel must have pushed me!

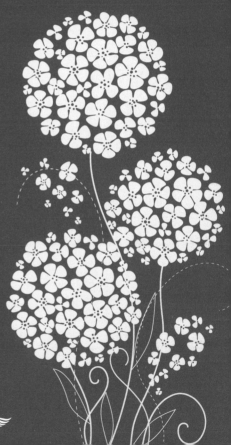

I had lain four months on my back in bed with my leg broken, and had so often dreamed that angels came and ministered to me that at the end of those four months the limb became as sound as though it had never been fractured.

Benvenuto Cellini

Many of the saints made it a practice never to undertake anything without first seeking the advice of their Guardian Angel.

St. Bernard of Clairveaux

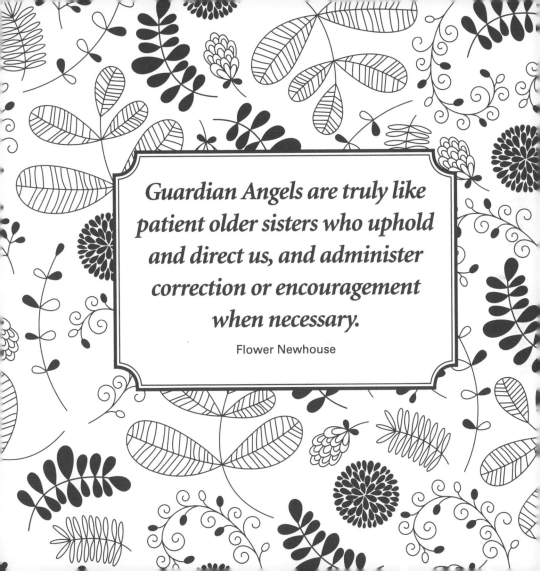

Guardian Angels are truly like patient older sisters who uphold and direct us, and administer correction or encouragement when necessary.

Flower Newhouse

BREAKING GLASS

My one-year-old son was in the kitchen, opening and closing the cabinet doors. I turned to get something from the pantry and heard a loud smashing noise. When I looked round, I saw that my son had pulled out two glass bowls which had smashed to the floor at his feet. I immediately picked him up and was amazed to see that he didn't even have a scratch. Glass had shattered everywhere around him, but he was untouched.

At that moment I truly believed in guardian angels.

A VOICE IN MY EAR

My belief in guardian angels began when I was traveling to a dental appointment at a city some sixty miles from my country home. I'd been awake all night getting my monthly publication ready for the printers. While driving along, I blinked my eyes to moisten them and apparently fell asleep at the wheel. Then I heard someone call my name three times, very urgently: 'Vivian, Vivian, Vivian!'

I opened my eyes immediately to find that I was on a curve on the highway. I could hear a 'tick, tick, tick' sound, regularly spaced, as my car either touched the guardrails or the grass beside them. Needless to say, I pulled over, got out of the car and danced around with my arms upraised saying: 'Thank you, Jesus!'

The guardian angels of life fly so high as to be beyond our sight, but they are always looking down upon us.

Jean Paul Richter

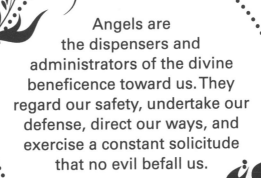

Angels are
the dispensers and
administrators of the divine
beneficence toward us. They
regard our safety, undertake our
defense, direct our ways, and
exercise a constant solicitude
that no evil befall us.

John Calvin

GOOD CATCH

When our church had a volunteer clean-up day, I helped by cutting overgrown vines out of the shrubs with a machete. About 15 feet away was an area where several young children were playing while their parents worked.

I was not experienced at using the machete and my hands were hot and sweaty. As I swung the machete across my chest, it flew out of my hands directly towards where the children were playing. I was horrified and prayed out loud,

'Lord, you are going to have to stop it – there is nothing I can do now!'

I ran towards where the children were playing, but I could not find the machete there. Then, with surprise, I spotted it lying near a tree some distance from the playground.

I believe an angel must have caught the spinning machete in the air near the children and placed it under the tree. Thanks to my guardian angel, none of the children was hurt.

The dignity of human
souls is great, for each
has an angel appointed
to guard it.

St. Jerome

*The wings of angels are often found on
the backs of the least likely people.*

Eric Honeycutt

Have you ever considered that, just perhaps, the reason you have gotten as far as you have is because of the invisible work of anonymous Angels? Good strangers in the night?

Gary Kinnaman

THE POWER OF PRAYER

My dad had been feeling unwell for some time and was receiving treatment for allergies. When he went to seek the opinion of a different doctor, he was told that his heart was five times its normal size and he should go to hospital right away. When he got there, the doctors tested him and prepared him for surgery. Afterwards the surgeon said my dad had the worst heart condition he had ever seen and he was surprised he had even made it to hospital!

While my dad was in recovery, a pastor who said he worked for the

hospital came in and asked if he could pray with him; my dad said that would be fine. Weeks later, when my dad had fully recovered and was leaving the hospital, he asked at the front desk if he could thank the pastor who had come in to pray with him. The woman at the desk searched on her computer, but could find no man with that name on the staff; nor had anyone of that name checked in to the hospital.

We know that an angel had come to pray with my dad that night, and had saved him.

When Britain first, at heaven's command,
Arose from out the azure main,
This was the charter of the land,
And guardian angels sung this strain:
'Rule, Britannia, rule the waves;
Britons never will be slaves.'

James Thomson

Communicating
with Angels

If trouble hearing Angels
song with thine ears,
try listening with thy heart.

Meriel Stelliger

Make yourself familiar
with the angels and
behold them frequently
in spirit; for without
being seen, they are
present with you.

St. Francis de Sales

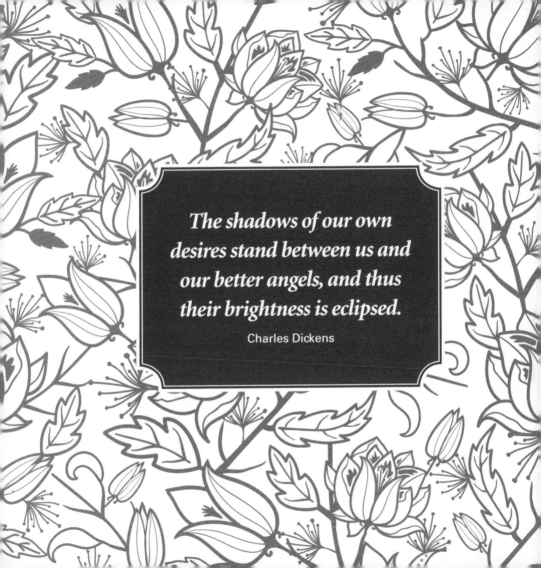

> *The shadows of our own desires stand between us and our better angels, and thus their brightness is eclipsed.*
>
> Charles Dickens

HITCHING A RIDE

I had left my job as a volunteer worker and was heading home where I was told a job was waiting for me. I had no money so decided to hitch. I found myself on a deserted highway. I couldn't see any gas stations or houses, and it was getting cold. I got on my knees and asked God to please help me.

While praying, I heard a car, and attempted to rise from my feet. Now this may be difficult to believe, but to this day I remember clearly feeling as though two hands were on my shoulders, preventing me from standing. Again I tried to stand, and again I felt a gentle but firm pressure on my shoulders and could not do it.

Now, if this was not amazing enough, I heard the car pulling over, its wheels crunching in the gravel on the side of the highway. On my third attempt to stand, I did so easily. A man got out of the car. I said in a loud voice, 'Thank you!' The man was obviously startled and said, 'Thanks for what?' He had apparently pulled over to obey the call of nature. I said, 'Thanks for pulling over to give me a ride,' to which he replied, 'I don't give people rides. I never have and I never will.' Sadly, I started off down the road, then heard him shout – 'But I will give you a ride!'

He told me that if I had stood up earlier he would never have pulled over, but would have continued down the highway. The thought occurred to me that truly a miracle had occurred and my prayer had been answered in a wonderful manner.

You don't need a formal prayer or invocation to call the Angels to your side. Simply think, 'Angels, please surround me', and they are there.

Doreen Virtue

The golden moments in the stream of life rush past us and we see nothing but sand; the angels come to visit us, and we only know them when they are gone.

George Eliot

Properly speaking, the angels
do not talk through their
assumed bodies; yet there is a
semblance of speech, in so far
as they fashion sounds in the
air like to human voices.

St. Thomas Aquinas

'HOW'S HEAVEN?'

When I was six, my nana passed away. It was really hard for me and my mom because we were both extremely close to her. But one night I went to sleep and dreamed a miracle!

In my dream, my family was hosting a party. So many people were there – aunts, uncles, grandparents, cousins and friends. The phone rang, so I picked it up and answered, 'Hello?'

The voice on the line said, 'Hi Madison, it's Nana!'

'Hi Nana', I said. 'How are you? How's heaven?'

'I'm great!', she answered. "Hey Madison, can you do me a favor? Can you tell your mom that I'm okay and I got to

heaven safely? I can see she has been a wreck and she's been praying a lot. Tell her I'm perfectly fine and happy in heaven and I'll see her when she comes up here.'

I told her I would; then I said goodbye and that I loved her, and hung up the phone.

The next morning I ran into my mom's room, bounced on her bed and said, 'Mom! Mom! Nana wants me to tell you that she's perfectly fine and happy and for you not to worry! She's safe with God.'

Mom was so confused! She had no idea what had happened. I told her my dream and to this very day, it is my favorite dream yet!

If you find it impossible to pray, charge your Good Angel to pray in your stead.

St. John Vianney

Becoming aware of our angels' hidden presence in our lives is not difficult or arduous, but it is subtle and requires great patience.

Eileen Elias Freeman

*All God's angels
come to us
disguised.*

James Russell Lowe

WEIRD VIBE

I was 20 years old when I moved out of my parents' house. My first apartment where I lived all alone had some weird vibe about it. One night I went to sleep, but woke up around 30 minutes later. I could feel someone staring at me.

A girl was standing next to my bed. Instead of feeling afraid, I felt a sense of complete calm.

The girl was wearing blue-and-white flannel pajamas; she was thin, bald and she had blue eyes. She said her name was Danielle and that she had died of leukemia in California at the age of 21. She sat on the edge of my bed and talked to me. She told me not to be afraid, that she was not there to take me. Then she told me to go back to sleep, and I lay back down and fell asleep.

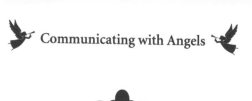

Oh passing angel, speed me with a song,
A melody of heaven to reach my heart
And rouse me to the race and make me strong.

Christina Rossetti

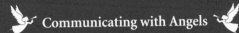

It is impossible to see the Angel
unless you first have a notion of it.

James Hillman

Be not forgetful to entertain
strangers, for thereby some have
entertained angels unawares.

Hebrews 13:2

A MESSENGER FROM GOD

One day I woke up feeling so depressed and suicidal that I decided the pain was too intense and I could no longer deal with it. I just wanted to die.

Nevertheless, I got up and went in to work. The whole day I kept thinking about what would be the least painful way to take my life. I decided to go to the local community college to enrol for a couple of classes to take my mind off things. But when I got there, the two classes I was interested in were full. Just my luck!

As I began walking back to my car, I started sobbing. The sun was setting and all I could see with my head down was people walking to and from their classes. All of a sudden, a beautiful young African-American woman

made her way through the crowd and on over to me. She grabbed hold of my arm and said these words: 'I have been sent here as a messenger from God.' Then she said my name: 'Rosemary, you are not going to go home and kill yourself. God has a plan for your life. He loves you and cares for you.'

I had never met this person before in my life. How did she know my name? So I asked her. She replied: 'I don't know your name, but He does, and He loves you very much.' She began talking to me and telling me about a bad relationship she had recently experienced with a boyfriend – and I felt as though I were listening to my own story or experience. This was amazing to me! From that day on, things began to change for the better.

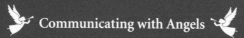
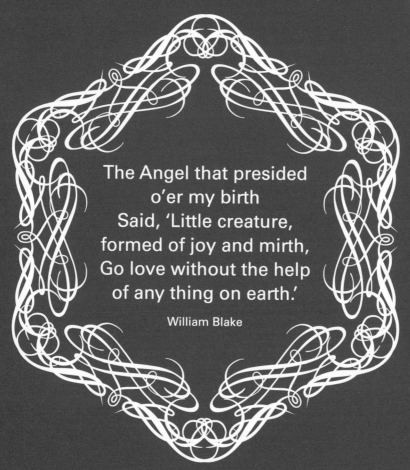

The Angel that presided
o'er my birth
Said, 'Little creature,
formed of joy and mirth,
Go love without the help
of any thing on earth.'

William Blake

Insight is better than eyesight when it comes to seeing an angel.

Eileen Elias Freeman

The angels are so enamored of the language that is spoken in heaven that they will not distort their lips with the hissing and unmusical dialects of men, but speak their own, whether there be any who understand it or not.

Ralph Waldo Emerson

ANGELIC SIGNALS

I was driving in my car thinking of God, so I decided to ask him, 'Do I have a guardian angel?'. At that very moment, I passed by a sign which read 'Angels'. Then, all of a sudden, a trail of ants came out of nowhere (I was in a car!) and went under my seat.

At a stoplight, I looked under the seat and found a mini-bible. I don't know how it got there or where it came from, but it was there. When I reached my destination I parked and opened the bible. It fell

open at page
22 where there was some
writing about how your angels are
always there. Now not only was that
freaky, but I was born at 2:22 a.m., and the
page was 22!

Driving back home, I asked if the angel
would play my favorite song on the
radio. The one that was playing at the
time stopped suddenly, and my favorite
song came on. It was a once in a lifetime
experience, and it changed my outlook
on everything.

Angels are messengers,
but sometimes we
misunderstand their
language.

Linda Solegato

Since God often
sends us inspirations
by means of
Angels, we should
frequently return our
aspirations to God by
means of the same
messengers.

St. Francis de Sales

Perhaps children's innocence, wherever it comes from, contributes to the fact that they seem to see angels more often.

John Ronner

JONESTOWN WARNING

Believe it or not, angels even yell sometimes! In September 1978, six friends were at the beach at Lummi Island razzing my friend Woody and his hippie buddy for saying, 'It will be cool to hang out with our two friends at Jonestown maybe a couple years.'

I was driving back to my Dad's house about three blocks away, when all at once there came a voice almost screaming, 'If Woody goes down there, he won't come back. He will die there!' It felt like the car was full of electricity. Three numbers, about three inches tall, plainly appeared at the top of the windshield: 9-2-0, with the voice, 'That is how many will die.'

When I got to the house I sat in my car for several minutes, unable to move. Then I said to my Dad and my stepmother, 'I just have to tell Woody.' When Woody came to help pull Dad's skiff up the beach, I told him what had happened. He said, 'I believe you' and then, of all things, 'but it might be OK anyway'! That is how we parted.

When the news about Jonestown appeared, I went through the list of 920 victims at least three times and did not see Woody's name. The following April he came walking down the beach and said, 'No big deal. We just decided we wouldn't go.'

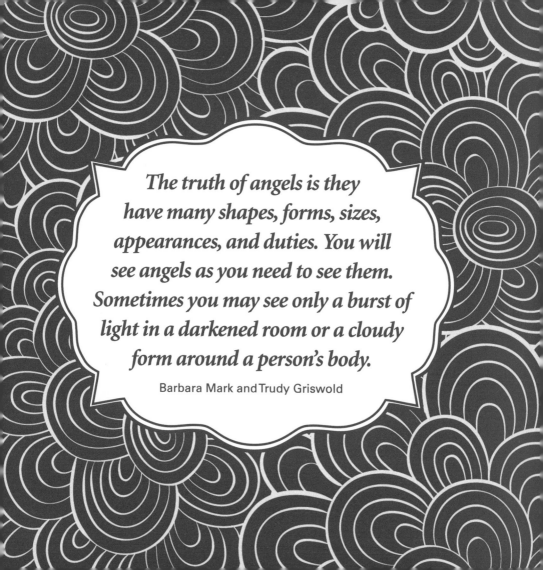

The truth of angels is they have many shapes, forms, sizes, appearances, and duties. You will see angels as you need to see them. Sometimes you may see only a burst of light in a darkened room or a cloudy form around a person's body.

Barbara Mark and Trudy Griswold

Though angels are both the messengers and the message of God, that makes them no easier to receive. For one thing, we almost never recognize them, even when they knock at our door.

F. Forrester Church

As the spirit blows where it will, so do angels ride the winds of spontaneity.

Maria Parisen

A TRAVELLING COMPANION

One of the most famous people to believe in angels is the current pontiff, Pope Francis. He told the crowds who gathered to celebrate the Feast of Holy Guardian Angels in 2014 that he considered his own guardian angel to be his 'travelling companion'.

He said: 'Often times, we have the feeling, "I shouldn't do this…this is not right…be careful". This is the voice of our guardian angel. Do not rebel: follow his advice. No one walks alone and none of us can think that he is alone, because this companion is always with us. It is dangerous to chase away our travelling companion, because no man, no woman can advise themselves.

I can give advice to another, but I cannot give advice to myself. The Holy Spirit [is] the angel who advises me. This is why we need him.'

Pope Francis suggested we should all ask ourselves the question: 'How is my relationship with my guardian angel? Do I listen to him? Do I wish him good morning? Do I say: "Protect me during sleep"? Do I speak with him? Do I ask his advice? He is at my side. We can respond to this question today, each and everyone of us: "How is my relationship with this angel who the Lord has sent to protect and accompany me along the way, and who always sees the face of the Father who is in the heavens?"'

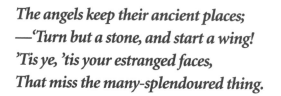

The angels keep their ancient places;
—'Turn but a stone, and start a wing!
'Tis ye, 'tis your estranged faces,
That miss the many-splendoured thing.

Francis Thompson

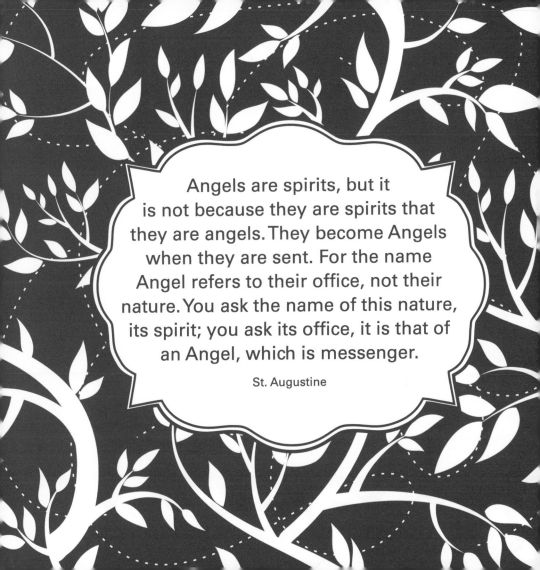

Angels are spirits, but it is not because they are spirits that they are angels. They become Angels when they are sent. For the name Angel refers to their office, not their nature. You ask the name of this nature, its spirit; you ask its office, it is that of an Angel, which is messenger.

St. Augustine

THE LOST MONEY ORDER

While relaxing in my mother in-law's back yard, I remembered I had left the money order for that month's rent in the back pocket of the jeans I had been wearing the previous day.

Upon arriving home, I immediately went upstairs to retrieve the order so I could mail it before it was late. I found my jeans and looked in all the pockets – no money order. I couldn't find it anywhere! My husband and I searched the entire house – all in vain.

I was devastated. At this time my husband was disabled, unable to work. I was the only one working. All I could think was that I had three beautiful young children who were going to be homeless if I didn't find that money order.

I got down on my knees at the side of our bed and prayed. I spoke to God and pleaded, 'Lord you know that I am trying…I cannot come up with this rent again. Please, Lord, help me find this money order.' On finishing my prayer, I opened my eyes. Then I saw the most amazing thing I have ever experienced in my entire life. On the bed, right in front of my eyes lay a white piece of paper. I reached for the paper, turned it over, and indeed it was the lost money order.

I am not crazy – I know this money order was not there before I knelt to pray. My guardian angel was there for me. I have never doubted the presence of higher beings since then. And never will!

THIRTEEN STOPS

We were on the outskirts of Paris, outside a bar where my friend was supposed to meet us. Only he wasn't there. All we had was the name of a hostel where we were staying. So we went down to the nearest metro. It was spooky, with not a soul in sight – no people, no trains.

It was getting late; the metro would be locked at midnight and there was no sign of the last trains. I thought, 'Great, our first night in Europe and we are going to be locked down here!' I said a little prayer to life. I said, 'Please help us out of this mess.'

Then, from out of nowhere, a little old Chinese woman appeared from a tunnel and walked towards us. I stopped her and showed her the name of the hostel. She smiled at me very graciously then, without words, she walked us through all these different tunnels and up onto a platform. She turned to me and said with her arm

outstretched, 'You take this train.' Just as she said this, the train pulled in and the door opened right behind her hand. I hardly had time to thank her, but I grabbed her warm hand and nearly cried with gratitude. 'Thirteen stops,' she said. I kept thanking her. But she just smiled and turned and walked back the way we had come.

I thought, 'If this is the last train, and she walked us ten minutes in the opposite direction to where she was going, and the metro is shut for the night, then where is she going?'

After thirteen stops, we got out, and there, right in front of us, was the hostel we were looking for.

I have always been grateful to that angel in Paris. I have every reason to believe that she vanished into thin air right after that. She's probably in this room as I write – smiling with me.

Make thine home, thine abode, where an angel would desire to visit, where an angel would seek to be a guest. For it will bring the greater blessings…

Edgar Cayce

So in a voice, so in a shapeless flame
Angels affect us oft, and worshipp'd be

John Donne

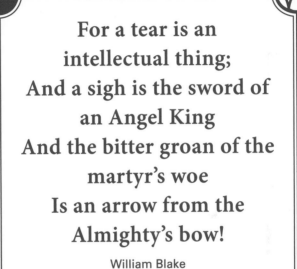

For a tear is an
intellectual thing;
And a sigh is the sword of
an Angel King
And the bitter groan of the
martyr's woe
Is an arrow from the
Almighty's bow!

William Blake

THE MAN IN WHITE

Mrs Richmond remembers when she was a young child on vacation in the rainforest of 'El Yunque' running after a beautiful butterfly and getting lost. She fell into a cave and hurt her leg. She tried to climb out, but couldn't, so she sat and cried, calling out for her parents.

She started to pray. She was terrified, cold and afraid of the bats which hung all around her. Then she heard the voice of a man calling out her name. She saw a shadowy figure climb into the cave. The man was smiling 'like nothing terrible had happened'. She felt relieved and asked if her parents were there; the man answered, 'No', but told her they were worried about her. She noticed that the man was dressed, not like a ranger, but all in white – t-shirt, pants, sneakers and hat. He picked her up as though she was light as a feather and carried her outside. He sat her on a rock and told her to wait. When she screamed for him not to go, he smiled and said, 'I will be back.'

After about ten minutes, she was found by rangers who took her to her worried parents. As they were getting ready to leave in their car, she said she wanted to wait 'for the nice man that saved her'. But the rangers said they had closed the path and no one could go in there. Her parents insisted that she needed to go hospital, so they left.

With a cast on her broken leg, she returned home two days later. One night, she heard someone calling her name from the yard. She looked out of her bedroom window and there was the man again, smiling and waving his hand. She tried to open the window but couldn't, and when she looked again, he was gone.

Angels are intelligent reflections of
light, that original light which has
no beginning. They can illuminate.
They do not need tongues or ears,
for they can communicate without
speech, in thought.

John of Damascus

*Then cherish pity, lest you drive
an angel from your door.*

William Blake

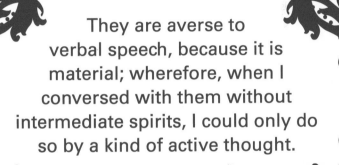

They are averse to
verbal speech, because it is
material; wherefore, when I
conversed with them without
intermediate spirits, I could only do
so by a kind of active thought.

Emanuel Swedenborg

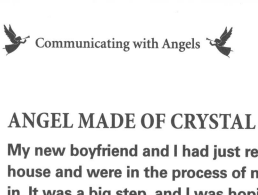

ANGEL MADE OF CRYSTAL

My new boyfriend and I had just rented a house and were in the process of moving in. It was a big step, and I was hoping I was making the right decision by moving in with my boyfriend after dating just a couple of months. I took a break from moving in our belongings and walked round the house, scanning the yard for heart-shaped rocks, which I collect. While I was picking up a few 'heart rocks' I spoke to God and 'the powers that be', asking for sign to let me know God and the angels were there and that I was making the right choice moving in with my boyfriend.

All of a sudden, something sparkly caught my eye. There, hanging on a scrap piece of wood leaning against the fence, was a crystal angel Christmas ornament. I was amazed and awestruck. I couldn't stop smiling and my heart was so full of happiness I felt like my chest would burst. I couldn't have asked for a more 'crystal clear' sign than that! Just to make sure I wasn't crazy, I took the ornament and asked my boyfriend and the friends who were helping us move if they had placed the ornament there. No one had seen it before, and when I told them my story they were just as amazed as I was. We took it to be a true sign from above, and this made me very happy!

Most accounts involve some wonderful or mysterious being who appeared when most needed and who was usually only recognized as an Angel in retrospect.

Ruth J. Moro

If you can't hear the angels, try quieting the static of worry.

Valentine Sterling

Divine Scripture from time to time introduces angels so apparent as to be seen commonly by all; just as the angels who appeared to Abraham were seen by him and by his whole family, by Lot, and by the citizens of Sodom; in like manner the angel who appeared to Tobias was seen by all present.

St. Thomas Aquinas

ON THE BEACH

Several years ago, while pregnant with my son, I went to the beach with my mother, grandmother and grandfather. I was going through a very hard time in my life. My husband was cheating on me, I was struggling financially, and my family did not know of my pregnancy.

I remember kneeling down, touching the water with my hands and feeling at such peace. I have always loved the ocean. I began to pray to God and ask for his help. I started crying because I felt very alone at the time, but quickly dried my tears so my family would not see.

When I was done praying, I stood up to find an older lady standing directly in front of me. She handed me a shell. I told her it was very pretty and handed it back to her. But she insisted that I take it. When I asked if she wanted me to keep it, I realized she could not speak English. I took the shell and thanked her. She smiled at me with a pleased look on her face.

I turned round and saw that my grandmother was standing close by. I showed her the shell, but when I turned back to point to the lady, she had disappeared. The only people on the beach that early morning were me, my grandmother, mother, grandfather and another couple. My grandmother and I were the only ones to see this lady. At that moment we both realized we had just witnessed an angel.

I feel the angel was letting me know I would not be alone on my journey.

It is to those who perceive through symbols, the poets, the artists, and seekers for meaning, that the angel makes himself known.

Theodora Ward

Ever felt an angel's breath in the gentle breeze? A teardrop in the falling rain? Hear a whisper amongst the rustle of leaves? Or been kissed by a lone snowflake? Nature is an angel's favorite hiding place.

Carrie Latet

Experiences with Angels do not occur to people by chance. There is a sort of run-up to the experience.

H.C. Moolenburgh

A BLINDING FLASH

When I was seven years old we went down to my nan and granddad's house to have a little bonfire night party.

I was standing on the patio near the door to the back garden. My dad was setting off the fireworks and they were beautiful. All of a sudden, an unbelievably bad feeling entered my gut and I wanted to shout 'Run!'. A spark from the bonfire must have got into the box of fireworks next to me and there was a blinding flash. I have no idea what happened next because I covered my eyes with my arms and all I could feel was my big coat

sleeves covering my face. I opened my eyes for a short period of time. Everywhere was white, it was windy as if I was standing on top of a mountain, and it was sort of slow motion. I heard this whizzing noise that got louder and louder, then stopped, and I opened my eyes to find I was still standing in the garden outside my grandparents' house. Shaking and scared, I had a terrified feeling, but not that bad gut feeling. I hadn't been harmed, nor had the rest of my family. I believe an angel had protected me for that short period of time.

The minute you speak
to your angel for the first time,
you will never be alone again,
because our angels are always with
us. No matter where you are as you
read this, you are surrounded by
angels. Your room, your office,
your garden, are filled with
angelic presences.

Eileen Elias Freeman

I throw myself down in my chamber, and I call in, and invite God, and his Angels thither, and when they are there, I neglect God and his Angels, for the noise of a fly, for the rattling of a coach, for the whining of a door.

John Donne

A GLOWING FIGURE

My mother was not religious, but I always saw something spiritual in her. In 1955 my brother was born premature and sickly. He only lived for about 18 months. My mom, being the mom she was, felt very guilty even though my brother's death was not her fault.

The night of his funeral she was lying in bed awake. Suddenly a large, white, glowing figure appeared in the closet door. My mom was not afraid. She woke up my dad, but he couldn't see anything. After the experience my mom no longer blamed herself for my brother's death and was at peace.

Unless you can love, as the angels may,
With the breadth of heaven betwixt you;
Unless you can dream that his faith is fast,
Through behoving and unbeloving;
Unless you can die when the dream is past —
Oh, never call it loving!

Robert Browning

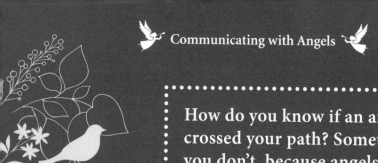
How do you know if an angel has crossed your path? Sometimes you don't, because angels often appear as coincidences.

Gary Kinnaman

Make friends with the angels, who though invisible are always with you. Often invoke them, constantly praise them, and make good use of their help and assistance in all your temporal and spiritual affairs.

St. Francis De Sales

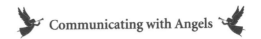

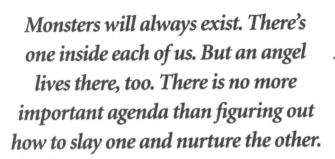

Monsters will always exist. There's one inside each of us. But an angel lives there, too. There is no more important agenda than figuring out how to slay one and nurture the other.

Jacqueline Novogratz

ANGEL ATTENDANT

One night, my boyfriend and I were leaving hospital after visiting a friend. My boyfriend had parked in the paid parking, but we didn't have any money to get out of the lot. We didn't know what to do. We sat in the car trying to figure out a way to sneak through the gate.

As time went on, we saw a man walking from out of nowhere. He didn't say a word to us: he just put money in the machine and we were able to get through the gate. Still not saying a word, we looked up to try to thank him, but within seconds he was gone. He vanished – and there were no cars in sight. An angel paid for us to exit the hospital parking lot!

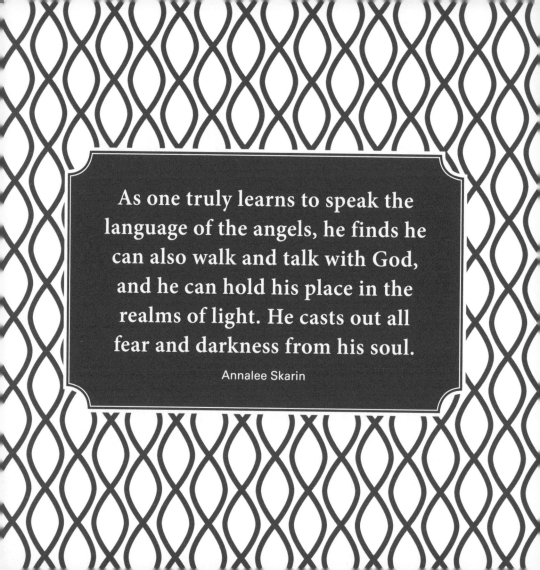

As one truly learns to speak the language of the angels, he finds he can also walk and talk with God, and he can hold his place in the realms of light. He casts out all fear and darkness from his soul.

Annalee Skarin

I have seen a thousand times that Angels are human form, or men, for I have conversed with them as man to man, sometimes with one alone, sometimes with many in company.

Emanuel Swedenborg

Whatever you put your attention on in this life will increase in your life. As you put your attention on angels, they will begin increasingly to make their presence known to you.

Denise Linn

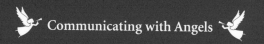

'THE LORD RELEASED ME...'

I was working on a commercial fishing anchor at Lummi Island, 60 feet beneath the ocean surface. One terrible day, I carelessly jammed a cable between the tank valve and the regulator. That left me held there with no air. After twisting every which way, I quit, saying – 'OK, Lord, if this is what you have planned for me, you know best' – and I passed out.

Of course, that should have been it. But the Lord released me. Upon waking I found I was whizzing up the anchor cable. About 15 feet from the surface, trying unsuccessfully to breathe again, I felt as though someone was right next to me. Then I heard a voice say: 'It is going to be all right.' Looking up at Tom Philpott's skiff,

I thought, 'I hope so.' The lights went out again and I floated to the surface.

When Tom got to me, my heart had stopped, my face was discolored and fluid was pouring from my nose and mouth. Tom had taken a CPR course a year earlier, so he quickly wiped some of the mess away, and I woke up with him puffing on my mouth.

A few days later, I was wondering why I had survived when others in similar situations had died. Then came that same voice again: 'You're not done here. There is something very special for you to do.'

Ask your angels to stay as near to you as they can; to help keep your vision clear and your presence simple, so in all the days to come there will be a radiance and Glory in your spirit.

Karen Goldman

Music is well said to be the speech of angels.

Thomas Carlyle

The Wisdom of Angels

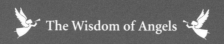

*Every man
contemplates an angel
in his future self.*

Ralph Waldo Emerson

To love for the sake of
being loved is human,
but to love for the sake
of loving is Angelic.

Alphonse de Lamartine

If a man is not rising upward to be an angel, depend on it, he is sinking downward to be a devil.

Samuel Taylor Coleridge

'DON'T WORRY ABOUT A THING...'

I had recently moved to New York City from Florida. I was going through a really difficult time because my mom and I are really close and I didn't want to leave her. As soon as I stepped onto the plane I felt as though something or someone was pushing me along, giving me strength. Even so, when I got to New York I cried myself to sleep for many nights. I continually doubted myself for moving and was a wreck emotionally.

Well, my boyfriend and I were at the train station one evening when he suddenly got the urge to pee, so he went to the bathroom in the station. I was standing outside waiting for him when a man approached me. He looked very strange and I thought he was going to ask me for money or hurt me. But as he got closer I saw that

he had a boombox around his neck and it was playing Bob Marley's song 'Three Little Birds', which goes: 'Don't worry about a thing – ' This made me smile. The man then looked me straight in the eyes and said, 'Life is good – don't worry, everything will work itself out and you will be all right.' My eyes filled with tears and I immediately took this as a sign from God.

A couple of seconds after the man had descended the stairs for the train, my boyfriend came out of the bathroom. I hurried him down the steps to see the man for himself, but the stranger was nowhere to be seen. This incident made me feel so much better, and I thank God and that angel with all my heart.

In poetry, no less than in life, he is 'a beautiful and ineffectual angel, beating in the void his luminous wings in vain'.

Matthew Arnold

An Angel can illumine the thought and mind of man by strengthening the power of vision, and by bringing within his reach some truth which the Angel himself contemplates.

St. Thomas Aquinas

*Heaven and earth
and all they hold:
angels, demons, and
men – it is I.*

Rumi

ANGELS ARE CAMPED AROUND YOU

I was a single parent at the time, and down to my last few cents. I found something of small value at home and decided to go to the local pawnshop with my youngest son. My oldest son was not with us. He had started really messing with drugs. As we entered the shop, a very beautiful, tall man walked over to us. He had dark, almond-coloured skin. His hair was long and in something like dreadlocks. His voice was otherworldly – refined and elegant.

He immediately started to tell me that my oldest son (who he called by name) was in God's hands and would be fine – he just had to go through what he was experiencing. He asked if he could pray for us. We were

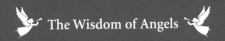

still just standing in the doorway, but I said that he could. He then handed me money and told me to leave. As we were driving off my son said: 'Look, Mom! The man disappeared! He must have been an angel!' I turned and looked – and he was gone.

For several years I tried looking everywhere for this man. My life had become easier and I had started on the road to where I am now (I'm an evangelist and a chaplain). One day my youngest son and I were in a different area, in a grocery store. A man walked up to my son…the same man as before! He started comforting my son and said some positive words to him.

Never give up. You must believe me – angels are camped around you.

To see the angel in the malady requires an eye for the invisible, a certain blinding of one eye and an opening of the other to elsewhere.

James Hillman

God and all angels sing the
world to sleep,
Now that the moon is rising
in the heat
And crickets are loud again
in the grass. The moon
Burns in the mind on lost
remembrances.

Wallace Stevens

MOTHER'S DAY ANGEL

In 2007 my husband and I lost our only son. It was a devastating time. He was only a month old when he passed. A week later, on Mother's Day, my parents were out of town and my husband was at work, also in another town. I went to the cemetery by myself. My son's headstone was not there yet. I was sitting by a pile of dirt, hunched over crying uncontrollably, when I felt someone wrap their arms around me and hug me.

I turned to find an older woman behind me. I said, 'This is my first Mother's Day and all I have is a pile of dirt!'

The woman told me things would be OK and that I'd make it through and would have another child. She walked away and came back with a rose. She said it was for my son, but she added she thought I needed it more. Then she left. I had not told her that I had a son.

I've been to the cemetery many times since then, but haven't seen her again. I don't know if she was an angel or not, but she was an angel to me! My husband and I now have a wonderful two-and-a-half-year-old child.

Time is man's angel.

Johann Christoph Friedrich von Schiller

But men must know, that in this theatre of man's life it is reserved only for God and angels to be lookers on.

Francis Bacon

Fools rush in where angels fear to tread.

Alexander Pope

ANGELS ON WHEELS

I was driving home from my friend's house. It had been my first visit – he lives about half-an-hour's drive from me. I have no sense of direction and get lost very easily. At that time there were no cell phones or computers. On the way, the highway split; I realized I had gone the wrong way when nothing looked familiar and I reached a long stretch of road with no service stations. I began to freak out and started praying for God to please help me find my way back home.

Shortly after I said the prayer, I saw a car pull over onto the hard shoulder some distance away. It was very late at night and there were no cars on the road. As I pulled up next to this car I saw an elderly couple inside it; they were sitting with the interior light on, reading a map. I couldn't believe my luck! I told them I was lost and needed to find Route 80-east. They said they were lost too, but suggested I follow them as they were going the same way as me.

I followed them until I saw signs I recognized, then quickly overtook them to beep and say thanks. But the car I was following was not them. I had been following a different car going in the same direction!

I believe my angels had disguised themselves as this couple so that I felt safe enough to approach them and ask directions to get home!

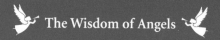
It is in rugged crises, in unweariable endurance, and in aims which put sympathy out of the question, that the angel is shown.

Ralph Waldo Emerson

Even the highest angels
seek out and learn
mysteries of grace.

St. Thomas Aquinas

I think it's obvious that
there is demon and angel
in all. And they are all
around us, too. It is like
beauty being in the eye of
the beholder.

Brychan Llyr

A BLESSING ON THE HIGHWAY

One evening, my husband and I went out for a meal. We noticed this elderly man watching us as though he wanted to say something. When he and his wife had finished their supper he came over to our table and said, 'I just want you to know that you will receive a blessing on the highway next week.' We said, 'thank you', but didn't think any more about it.

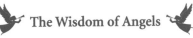

The following week our son was coming home. While driving at about 100mph, something told him to slow down – so he did. At that moment, a tire and rim blew off the jeep he was driving, but the vehicle didn't flip or roll over. Our son was able to stop and walk to the first exit to call home for help. I know that his angel had kept the jeep from flipping over. We never saw the elderly man and his wife again.

Smells are the
fallen angels of
the senses.

Helen Keller

Neither man nor angel can discern
Hypocrisy, the only evil that walks
Invisible, except to God alone,
By His permissive will, through
heav'n and earth.

John Milton

*O, what may man
within him hide,
Though angel on the
outward side!*

William Shakespeare

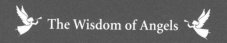

'YOU ARE NOT ALONE...'

I went through a life-shattering divorce soon after the birth of my son. I was living in Atlanta, Georgia, at the time, and my family was living in Chicago. My husband had left several weeks earlier and I was getting ready to move out. I had loaded my things onto a removal truck and was spending the last few days with my infant son at a girlfriend's house. I was selling our house and moving back to Chicago. It was a very dark time.

My friend dropped us at the airport and we said goodbye. I was leaving so much behind: my marriage, my friends, my home and my job. I felt so alone as she drove away.

I put my son in his stroller and began walking down the sidewalk to the terminal. As I was walking along, I felt two firm taps on my shoulder. I turned round quickly only to find that no one was there. No one was even near me! At that very second I heard the words, 'You are not alone.' These words were not audible – they came as a loud inner voice, but it was not my own 'thinking voice'. The taps were as real as anything, though – so firm that they were just shy of uncomfortable.

A feeling of love swept over me. I smiled and was reassured, and boarded the plane feeling much lighter. I have not felt alone in that way since then.

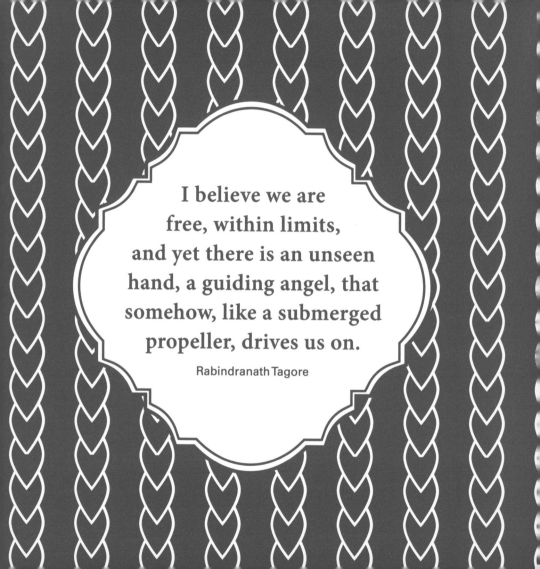

I believe we are
free, within limits,
and yet there is an unseen
hand, a guiding angel, that
somehow, like a submerged
propeller, drives us on.

Rabindranath Tagore

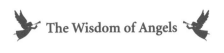
Angels deliver Fate to our doorstep –
and anywhere else it is needed.

Jessi Lane Adams

The Present, the Present
is all thou hast
For thy sure possessing;
Like the patriarch's angel
hold it fast
Till it gives its blessing.

John Greenleaf Whittier

OVER THE TANNOY

It was Saturday morning at Kellingley colliery in North Yorkshire. The weekend was the time when coal production stopped and much-needed maintenance work was carried out. Harry was above ground, assisting a young electrician deep underground who was installing a 100-metre, high-voltage cable. Once the cable was installed, Harry knocked the switch off and told the young electrician to test the cable. But Harry had thrown the wrong switch and the cable was still live (11,000 volts).

After Harry finished his phone call to the young electrician, a voice came over the mine's Tannoy system. It asked Harry to check that the power really was

switched off. Harry said he was sure it was, but the voice
was insistent and told him to check it. Harry casually
checked the power and found it was still on! With his
heart pounding, he ran to throw the correct switch – with
seconds to spare!

The incredible thing about this incident is that the Tannoy
was not connected to the mine's power supply. In fact, it
was going to be Harry's job to connect it the following
week! Harry believes that he spoke to a guardian angel
that day, who saved the lives of all the men in the mine
and saved him from ruining his own life.

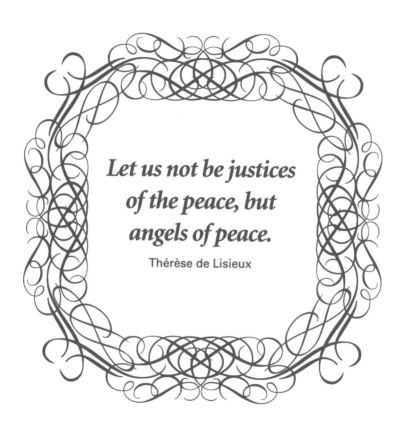

Let us not be justices of the peace, but angels of peace.

Thérèse de Lisieux

Keep your good deeds for others a secret, just as your Angel works behind the scenes in your own life.

Eileen Elias Freeman

Angels can fly because they take themselves lightly.

G.K. Chesterton

A VOICE IN MY EAR

I was driving home from work alone
on a winding, hilly two-lane highway
in Tennessee, day-dreaming as usual.
All of a sudden, I heard a voice say
clearly, 'Slow down!' I thought, 'Did
I really hear that?' The voice came
again, louder. I heard it in my ears,
not in my head: 'Slow down!!'

I have never before heard voices
in my life. This one was distinctly

male and authoritative. I braked
and slowed down to about 35mph.
I went on for about a quarter of a
mile, over a couple of hills and round
curves. As I came up over another
rise, there was a car overtaking
the car coming toward me; it was
in my lane and completely across
the double yellow line. If I hadn't
listened to the voice, I would have
hit that car head on.

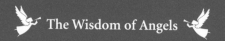
Our acts our angels are, for good or ill,
Our fatal shadows that walk by us still.

John Fletcher

A man does not
have to be an
angel in order to
be a saint.

Albert Schweitzer

Via the angel we glimpse
the unknown, and we are
encouraged to press on.

Rosemary Ellen Guiley

THE MYSTERY SLED

During World War II my mother and my brother were refugees in Russia, having fled from the Nazis in Poland. My mother did everything she could to feed them both. She traded goods on the black market for some material, which she hoped to exchange for food at a nearby farm.

When she reached the farm, the people were very kind. They fed her and filled her small sled with grains and vegetables. She was elated. But on the way home it started to snow so heavily that the sled got stuck, and my mother couldn't move any further. 'God,' she prayed, 'what will happen to my little boy? Please protect him.'

Suddenly, a large horse-drawn sled appeared. The driver had a fur rug covering his legs and ice hanging from his handlebar moustache. He hooked up my mother's sled and drove her right up to her door. My mother took her things inside, but when she turned round to invite him in for some hot tea, he had gone. No trace of him could be found.

My mother is convinced that he was her angel and the answer to her prayer – and so am I.

> It is not because angels are holier than men or devils that makes them angels, but because they do not expect holiness from one another, but from God only.
>
> William Blake

Ambition first sprung
from your blest abodes;
The glorious fault of angels
and of gods.

Alexander Pope

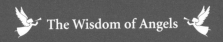

Give of yourself as the Angels do, and wonderful things will come to you.

Ramadan

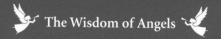

ANGEL IN THE DOORWAY

My mom is sure that after my brother died at 18 months of age she saw an angel who helped her through it. On the night of my brother's funeral, my mom had gone to bed feeling distressed and guilty that she had not been able to protect her baby. He had been born too early and was ill. That night, while lying in bed, my mom saw a large, white, glowing figure in the bedroom doorway. After this encounter she felt at peace and no longer blamed herself for her baby's death.

Then, in 2001, my mom passed away suddenly. About three days before she died, she asked my sister why she had been in her room at 3 a.m. My sister lives 88 miles away. My mom insisted that she had seen my sister standing by her door. We believe that this was an angel coming to lead mom to heaven. Perhaps it was my brother?

The virtue of angels is that
they cannot deteriorate;
their flaw is that they cannot
improve. Man's flaw is that he
can deteriorate; and his virtue
is that he can improve.

The Talmud

But sad as angels for the
good man's sin,
Weep to record, and blush
to give it in.

Thomas Campbell

Could we forbear dispute
and practise love,
We should agree as angels
do above.

Edmund Waller

A BRIGHT LIGHT

My parents both died three years ago, just four months apart. My mother was diagnosed with cancer the day after my dad was buried. It was a shock and she was devastated; not only had she lost her husband of 57 years, she would not live to see my children grow up. She was not ready to die. The months passed, and I mourned terribly for both of them. I prayed and prayed for a sign that they were OK, and that they knew I could be OK.

The night before last, I was asleep in my bed. My five-year-old son had

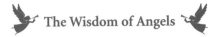

climbed in bed with us. We have an old lamp by the bed that won't turn on easily. In the middle of the night I was awakened suddenly by a bright light. When I sat up I saw that the old lamp was on, and shining so bright it was blinding. I reached over and shut it off so as not to wake my son. I lay back down puzzled, and looked at my alarm clock – it was 3:38 a.m. Then I realized the date was January 21. The exact date and time of my mother's death, three years ago.

I suddenly felt like my chest was full and my heart was going to burst right out. I realized my mother had come to let me know she was OK, and that I should be too. I will never ever forget that feeling, or forget the brightness of that light.

Lost Angel of a ruined Paradise!
She knew not 'twas her own; as
with no stain
She faded, like a cloud which had
outwept its rain.

Percy Bysshe Shelley

Individuals do not meet by chance. They are necessary in the experiences of others, though they may not always use their opportunities in a spiritual way or manner.

Edgar Cayce

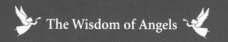
THE LADY WITH WHITE HAIR

I would like to share a story that happened to my sister Lisa's son, Joel.

My grandmother had passed on almost ten years ago, and Joel had never met her. One night Joel said to his mother, 'Mom, please get me that teddy bear', but Lisa was not tall enough to reach it down from the top shelf. She said, 'We will get it down for you

tomorrow', then tucked him into bed.

The next day Lisa went into the room to get Joel up for school and saw the teddy bear in bed with him. She said, 'Who gave that to you?'. Joel was only six years old at the time and there was nothing for him to climb on. Joel said, 'The lady with the white hair gave it to me.'

My grandmother had white hair.

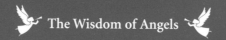
Pride still is aiming at the blest abodes,
Men would be angels, angels would be gods.

Alexander Pope

It can in no sense be said that heaven is outside of any one; it is within…and a man also, so far as he receives heaven, is a recipient, a heaven, and an angel.

Emanuel Swedenborg

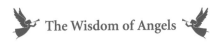

But till we are built like angels –
with hammer and chisel and pen,
We will work for ourself and a
woman, for ever and ever, amen.

Rudyard Kipling

DREAM ANGEL

My mom always said that if you dreamed of the dead, you heard from the living.

My brother died three years ago. I had never dreamed of him until just a week ago. In my dream, I was standing on my mom's front porch. I saw my brother walking down the steps and I called out to him, asking him why he had come back. He turned and smiled at me, then said he had to go down the street to his house to talk to his wife, Kathy. I asked him again why he had come back, and he

said, 'To get Kathy'. I asked him if he would be coming back again and he said he would see me soon.

Three days later, Kathy had just visited my brother's grave and was going to the store when she was hit by a car and killed instantly.

I believe my brother had been preparing me for this. I know now that angels can come in any form to us and somehow comfort us when things happen over which we have no control.

That's all an angel
is, an idea of God.

Meister Eckhart

Man is made a little lower than the angels, and yet with the ability of choice, and thus may turn those conditions or positions or associations into hell or heaven, according to the use of same.

Edgar Cayce

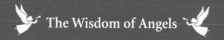
IN A BETTER PLACE

My grandfather had been fighting stomach cancer for years, but on March 21, 2006, the battle ended for him. Before he died, my mom had been to visit him. She told him she would be fine after his death if he could give her a sign telling her that he was OK.

About two weeks later, my mom was at work and the song 'Angel' by Sarah McLachlan came on the radio. A ray of sunshine fell across my mom's face and she turned to her co-worker and told her she thought her dad

had just passed away. Five minutes later, she got a call from her sister saying that their dad had died.

We said our sad goodbyes, but we knew he wasn't in pain any more and that he was in a better place. On the one-year anniversary of his death, my mom was at work and the same song, 'Angel', came on the radio. My mom noticed that it was at the exact time of day her dad had died. She got goose bumps and looked up and said, 'Thank you, dad'.

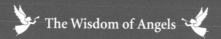
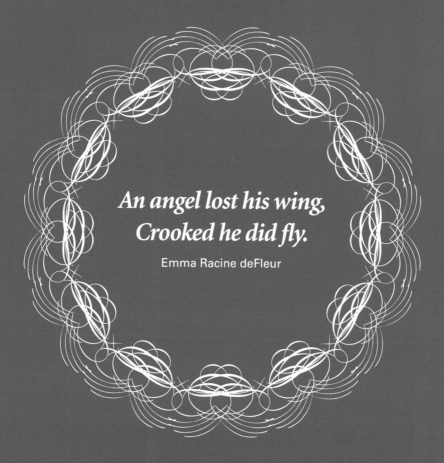

An angel lost his wing,
Crooked he did fly.

Emma Racine deFleur

He spake well who said that graves are the footprints of angels.

Henry Wadsworth Longfellow

Angels exist through the eyes of faith.

Reverend John Westerhoff

'YOU WILL GET THROUGH ALL THIS...'

I was sitting watching television one evening and feeling down since I was going through a divorce. My little nine-month-old boy had a flu bug and I had been up for what seemed like 24 hours. Suddenly I heard a noise coming from my room, where he had been sleeping, so I went to the door to take a peek at him. My mouth fell open and I stood frozen to the spot. What appeared to be an angel was walking out of my closet through the closed door.

He looked right at me and said, 'Do not be afraid, you will get through all this, and your son will be well and will grow to tell of me.' As I stood there, not knowing what to do, he disappeared.

I ran to the bed where my son was sleeping to make sure he was all right, then went to the phone to call my mom. I explained what had just happened, thinking she must think I was going mad. She rushed over to my house, and just by looking at me knew that I had been shaken by what had happened. She tried to reassure me by saying that angels can come to a person in times of need.

My son recuperated from the flu and my divorce turned out not to be as messy as expected. I thanked that angel over and over for blessing me.

But we can all be angels to one another. We can choose to obey the still small stirring within, the little whisper that says, 'Go. Ask. Reach out. Be an answer to someone's plea.'

Joan Wester Anderson

Philosophy will clip an angel's wings.

John Keats

Reputation is what men and women think of us. Character is what God and the angels know of us.

Thomas Paine

Angels are as real as the people in another town or country whom we cannot see, but whose existence we accept. We form an opinion about them from what we read and hear. Sometimes we meet them in person. Just so with the angelic forces.

Eleanore Mary Thedick

The Joy of Angels

AN ANGEL BROKE MY FALL

I needed to fix the covering on my furnace pipe, which was located on the roof. As I stepped on the top rung of the ladder, it slid from under me. I fell off, but in the split second before I hit the ground I felt what was like two hands grabbing my shoulders. I landed perfectly on my feet, as though I had been gently lowered down. I give thanks every day I'm alive and I try to make the world a better place with my own actions.

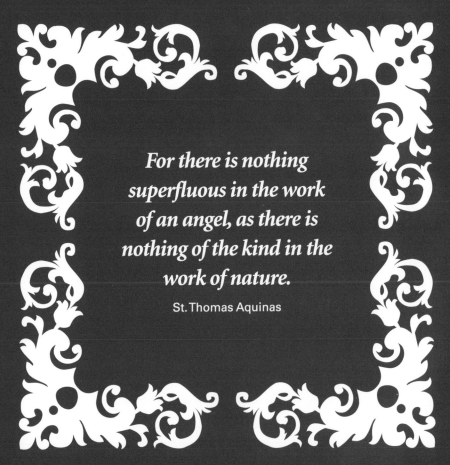

For there is nothing superfluous in the work of an angel, as there is nothing of the kind in the work of nature.

St. Thomas Aquinas

We are each of us angels with only one wing. And we can only fly by embracing each other.

Luciano de Crescenzo

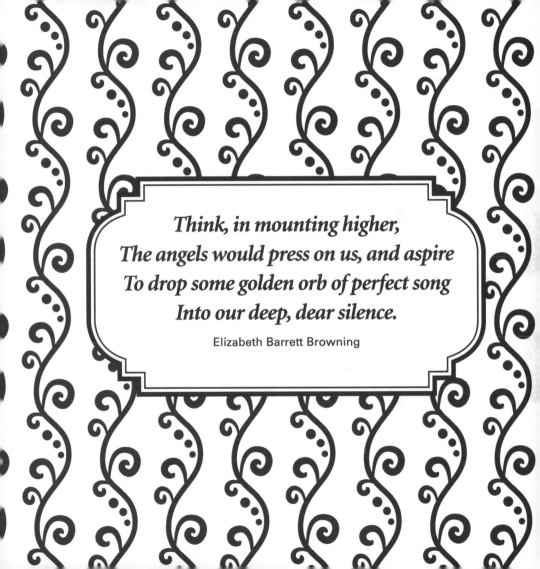

Think, in mounting higher,
The angels would press on us, and aspire
To drop some golden orb of perfect song
Into our deep, dear silence.

Elizabeth Barrett Browning

AN ANGEL IN PRISON

My story takes place when I was serving a 12-month sentence in prison. While I was in there during that long year, I was losing my mind. I was missing my family. I was missing my freedom. It felt as though I was never going to get out of there.

One day, around noon, I was lying on my bed when all of a sudden the electricity went out. It was pitch black. All I could hear was other inmates screaming and kicking doors. I couldn't see, my heart started racing and I began to panic. I closed my eyes and prayed to God for help. When I opened my eyes, there was this bright light shining into my cell from under the door. It was unbelievably bright. So I got up from my bed and went to the window in the door and looked through it. There was nothing but darkness on the other side. I looked down at the bottom of the door and there was the light, still shining very brightly into my cell.

I sat back down on my bed and stared at the light. Suddenly I was calm and something in my head told me, 'patience'. About five minutes later, the electricity came back on. And while everyone else was screaming with joy and cussing at the guards, all I could think was: 'Was that an angel? Was that a sign from God telling me to have patience?' I thanked God, and from that day I trusted in Him.

It's been five years since my release and I'm currently at college majoring in computer technology. My heart is pure; it's brand new. Sometimes it takes a painful experience to help you change your ways.

Good night, sweet prince, and flights of angels sing thee to thy rest!

William Shakespeare

Silently, one by one,
in the infinite
meadows of heaven,
Blossomed the lovely
stars, the forget-me-
nots of the angels.

Henry Wadsworth Longfellow

328

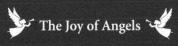

In Heaven, an
angel is nobody
in particular.

George Bernard Shaw

A WHOLE HOST OF ANGELS

I was standing in line at the dollar store. It's a very busy place these days as there are so many people who have fallen on hard times.

As my purchases were being rung up, I looked at the customer in the next lane. Her face was sad and drawn and looked gray – like she was sick. She seemed defeated and heavy with grief. I did something I've never done before. I asked my angels to wrap the stranger in love and lift her up, to hug and kiss her and make her feel delightfully happy and as light as a feather. I asked them to fill her with joy and make her laugh. I also asked for her to be healed of whatever was making her look so gray. I imagined the angels surrounding her.

Right before my eyes, the corners of her mouth started to lift! I quickly glanced away so she wouldn't see me looking at her, and then I heard laughter! Loud laughter! I looked over, and she was laughing and saying to the cashier, 'Do you know what I'm going to do? I'm going to go out to eat!!' Then she practically skipped out of the store. As she passed me, I saw that her skin was healthy and pink. I watched her drive away, beaming with joy, and I prayed that her angels would keep her wrapped in love and fill her with faith that everything would be all right.

My grandmother told me that every one of us has a whole host of angels from heaven surrounding us, and they will do what we ask. I believe it is true!

When we freely forgive others who have hurt us, our angel brings us a special blessing of love.

Eileen Elias Freeman

Were we as eloquent as angels we still would please people much more by listening rather than talking.

Charles Caleb Colton

 The Joy of Angels

We trust in plumed procession,
For such the angels go —
Rank after Rank, with even feet
And uniforms of Snow.

Emily Dickinson

SUDDEN JOY

One night, as I was lying in bed depressed and unhappy, I felt a sudden, inexplicable joy in my heart. I also heard a choir singing. This experience has occurred twice in my life. I thank you, Lord, for always sending me angels to help me in times of need. Thank you, my cosmic friends from the light. I appreciate your presence and help.

Angels sail back to God
on the sea of joy.

Adeline Cullen Ray

If instead of a gem, or even a flower, we
should cast the gift of a loving thought
into the heart of a friend, that would be
giving as the angels give.

George MacDonald

Have you ever seen a flower down
Sometimes angels skip around
And in their blissful state of glee
Bump into a daisy or sweet pea?

Jessi Lane Adams

DEEP WATER

Our pastor had taken his family to the coast for a well-deserved holiday. The adults were sitting on the beach and the kids were playing in the waves. Their eldest girl (a teenager) went in deeper than the rest and was swimming just behind the breakers. The tide grabbed her and within minutes she was dragged out into very deep water.

People saw what was happening and started shouting for the lifeguards. Thirty-five minutes later, the girl was dragged out onto the beach. She had a remarkable story to tell. According to her, as the current got hold of her, she could feel herself being dragged deeper and could see the

people on the beach getting smaller. As she tried to fight the tide and swim back to shore, a man appeared next to her. He said that all she was doing was tiring herself out. He told her to calm down and stop trying to fight the current. He was a young man with long blond hair, but he had a full white beard.

Once she had calmed down, the young man told her he couldn't help her, but he would stay with her till the lifeguards arrived. After she had been rescued and was safely on dry land, she asked for the blond man in order to thank him. But the lifeguards said she had been the only person in the sea when they found her.

If an angel were
ever to tell us
anything of his
philosophy, I believe
many propositions would
sound like two times
two equals three.

Georg C. Lichtenberg

And the Angel said, 'I have learned that every man lives, not through care of himself, but by love.'

Leo Tolstoy

'YOU HAVE GOT TO BELIEVE...'

When I was 19 years old I was very much in love with Steven, my boyfriend at the time. We had broken up and I was devastated. I was sitting outside my dentist's office, waiting for my sister (who was late), crying inconsolably.

All of a sudden I felt someone tap me on the shoulder. As I looked up I was taken aback because in front of me was standing this dishevelled-looking man. I guess he saw how shocked I was and he spoke these words: 'My dear, everything in your life will turn out OK. You will have

a son and name him Paul, and he will be very special.'
When I looked up again, the man was gone.

Nine years later, I had the most beautiful baby boy you
can imagine. I named him Paul, not because of the angel
but because this was his father's name. After the birth my
dad said, 'Remember what that man told you all those
years ago about having a son and naming him Paul? All
I'm trying to say is that there really are angels out there –
you have got to believe.'

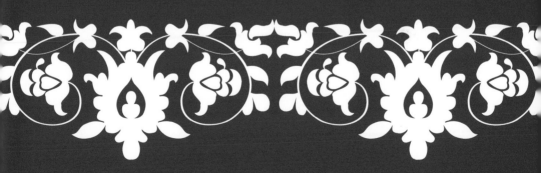

In the case of those who are making progress from good to better, the good angel touches the soul gently, lightly, sweetly, as a drop of water enters a sponge.

St. Ignatius of Loyola

The angels see you as dazzling young diamonds which are being polished to perfection.

Elsa Joy Bailey

You'll meet more angels on a winding path than on a straight one.

Daisey Verlaef

THREE ANGELS

I prayed to God that I would see a feather, so I'd know if my angel was present. If ever I forgot my request, I asked God to remind me that when I see a feather it is my angel.

One night I dreamt of three angels who appeared to me outside my room. It was so peaceful. The first angel was blurred; I didn't see its face clearly, but in my heart I knew it was an angel. The second angel was like Cupid – a cute, chubby little angel, and he was smiling at me. The third was a girl – she was wearing a white robe. Her wings and her whole body were so shiny that they radiated light.

In my dream I was so happy to see them because they bring peace and happiness. When I woke up the next morning, I was smiling because of my dream. God didn't grant my feather request, but what He let me experience was more than I asked for. He let me encounter angels and see them personally, in my dreams.

If I have freedom in my love,
And in my soul am free;
Angels alone, that soar above,
Enjoy such liberty.

Richard Lovelace

O lyric Love, half-angel and half-bird
And all a wonder and a wild desire.

Robert Browning

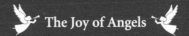
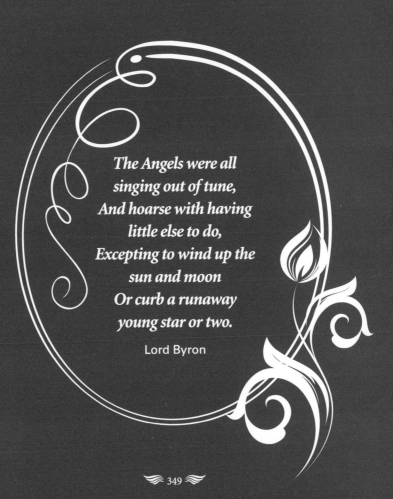

The Angels were all
singing out of tune,
And hoarse with having
little else to do,
Excepting to wind up the
sun and moon
Or curb a runaway
young star or two.

Lord Byron

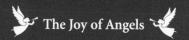
YELLOW BUTTERFLY

When my boyfriend and I were planning our wedding, my grandmother became ill. On her deathbed, she asked my boyfriend to promise to bring God into my life. He said he would, and he has fulfilled that promise.

On the day of our wedding, a yellow butterfly was seen during the whole ceremony (which was held in my parents' back yard). During important parts of the ceremony, the butterfly landed on my butt! We thought it was pretty funny – nothing could stop it going right back! After the wedding, we greeted our guests and kept seeing that butterfly around us. We all made jokes about it. Then, while the photographer was taking pictures, the butterfly landed on my husband's shoulder. We have a picture of him smiling with a bright yellow butterfly beautifully positioned on his shoulder. We never thought too much of it.

We have been married almost seven years now. It seems that every time I cry out for God to help me through a crisis, I look up and see a bright, beautiful, yellow butterfly. I have seen it more than 100 times during my marriage. I cannot remember ever seeing one at all until my wedding day.

All I know is that I love that yellow butterfly. To me, it means, 'Everything is going to be all right.'

I will not wish thee riches, nor the glow
of greatness,
But that wherever thou go some weary
heart shall gladden at thy smile,
Or shadowed life know sunshine for a
while.
And so thy path shall be a track of light,
Like angels' footsteps passing through
the night.

Words on an English church wall

It is not known precisely where the angels dwell – whether in the air, the void, or the planets. It has not been God's pleasure that we should be informed of their abode.

Voltaire

If I got rid of my demons, I'd lose my angels.

Tennessee Williams

A PRECIOUS GIFT

On January 27, 2004, I was given one of the most precious gifts I've ever received from a total stranger. This gift was the feathers of an angel.

The stranger was an elderly woman who had come into my store on this day. Her husband had recently passed away. He had feared leaving his wife alone because she walked with a cane and he worried about how she would get along without him.

One evening, while she was visiting him in hospital, he asked her if she could see the angels in the room. She said, 'No, but if you say they are here, I believe you.'

Then her husband motioned toward the floor. There were feathers all around the bed.

To this day, the lady finds feathers around her home. She picks them up each day, only to find more the next day.

One day, she had to pay her water bill, but could see from her bank statement that she did not have enough money to pay it. She called her bank to verify her balance. To her surprise she was told she had $600 in her account. No recent deposit had been made. She looked down at the bank statement and there were new white feathers where none had been only moments before.

I believe – do you?

You can become what you want. You have an army of angels behind you.

Sue Fitzmaurice

I am a little world made cunningly
Of elements, and an angelic sprite.

John Donne

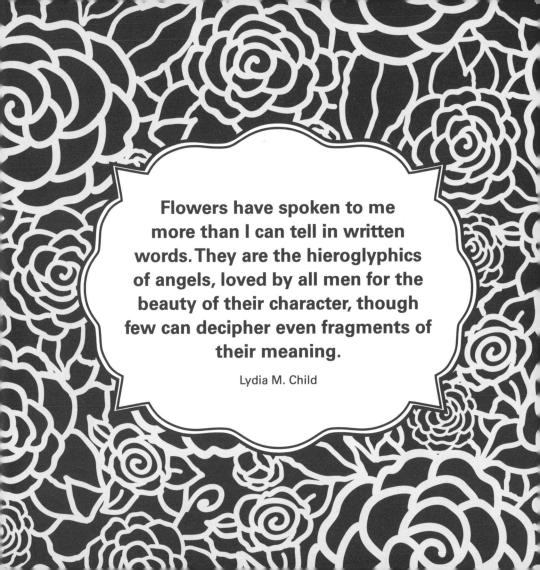

Flowers have spoken to me more than I can tell in written words. They are the hieroglyphics of angels, loved by all men for the beauty of their character, though few can decipher even fragments of their meaning.

Lydia M. Child

MR LUCKY

My wife and I checked in to a motel for the night. As we started up the stairs to the second floor, I looked across the parking lot and saw an old man rummaging around in a dumpster. I ran back down the stairs and over to the man.

'Please don't do that', I said. I reached in my pocket and took out two rolls of quarters. 'Here – please take this and get yourself something to eat.' 'Thank you, Mr Lucky', the man said, in a soft tone.

My wife and I went to our room. After about 30 minutes I looked over at her and said, 'I would really like to play cards.' We put on our coats and went over to the casino.

I sat there for six hours, winning. When the game was finally over I had won over $16,000 – more money than I had ever seen in my entire life. My wife and I decided

to quit while we were ahead. As we were leaving the casino, we saw the old man from the parking lot; he was standing by the front door, out in the cold.

'Can I buy you a drink?' I asked him.

The old man reached out and touched me gently on the forehead. A very strange, warm feeling came over my entire body – a calmness like I had never known. 'I don't drink, Mr Lucky', he said, smiling at me. I held out a $100 bill, but he did not take it. He turned round and walked away into the night.

That was almost 25 years ago this November. I have recently survived a near-fatal illness – two years ago the doctor gave me less than six months to live, but I'm still here! I now know what the old man meant when he called me 'Mr Lucky'.

The Joy of Angels

I feel that there is an angel inside me whom
I am constantly shocking.

Jean Cocteau

Philosophers have argued for centuries about how many angels can dance on the head of a pin, but materialists have always known it depends on whether they are jitterbugging or dancing cheek to cheek.

Tom Robbins

I never wanted a guardian angel.
I didn't ask for one.
One was assigned to me.

Mercedes McCambridge

A BLUR OF WHITE LIGHT

When I was four years old, I was in my mother's bedroom. I saw a bottle with some orange liquid in it on the dresser. I was thirsty and I thought it was orange juice, so I climbed up onto the dressed and drank from the bottle.

I became sick, then passed out and was rushed to hospital. All I can remember is this blur of

white light in the room. Two angels were standing next to Jesus, who told me that I could not stay with them; it was not time. He said I needed to stay on Earth to help people and to live my life – to get married, have children and have a job.

I was taken down to Earth again by the two angels. It felt as though I was pulled back into my body with a rush of air. I was alive – I made it!

'SHE IS SAFE...'

My wife and I had two children, Jennifer and Natasha, born a year apart. Natasha died when she was less than a year old. Jennifer was in a great deal of pain and torment about this.

One day, when she was about five years old, Jennifer saw a radiant looking lady who appeared at the foot of her bed. The lady said: 'You don't have to worry about your sister any more – she is safe in her Father's arms.'

After this, Jennifer was less troubled; she was able to cope with the loss of her sister.

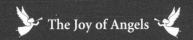

The reason why birds can fly and we can't is simply that they have perfect faith, for to have faith is to have wings.

J.M. Barrie

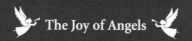
The Joy of Angels

To marry is to domesticate the Recording Angel. Once you are married, there is nothing left for you, not even suicide, but to be good.

Robert Louis Stevenson

Flag of the free heart's hope
and home!
By angel hands to valor given;
Thy stars have lit the welkin dome,
And all thy hues were born
in heaven.

Joseph Rodman Drake

The more materialistic science becomes, the more angels shall I paint. Their wings are my protest in favour of the immortality of the soul.

Edward Burne-Jones

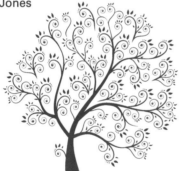

Outside the open window
The morning air is all
awash with angels.

Richard Wilbur

. . . her angel's face
As the great eye of heaven shinéd bright,
And made a sunshine in the shady place;
Did never mortal eye behold such
heavenly grace.

Edmund Spenser

PENNIES FROM HEAVEN

Several years ago, my husband and I were having serious financial problems. We had two sons to provide for – I was not working and my husband had lost his job. He found another, but it didn't pay very much.

One day, we were out of food. We had no money and my husband was not due to be paid for several days. I was very worried about how we would feed our kids. I got up from the couch in the living room, went to the window and just stared outside. It was a chilly, windy day. All of

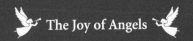

a sudden, my eyes came to rest on something on the front lawn – it looked like money.

I ran outside as fast as I could and found that it was two $20 bills folded together. I was so thrilled, I went straight to the grocery store and bought some food to sustain us until pay day. I couldn't understand why the money hadn't blown away in the wind. It had just lain there on the grass. It took me a while to realize that an angel must have been guarding the money and preventing it from blowing away.

Look how the floor of Heaven
Is thick inlaid with patines of bright gold
There's not the smallest orb that thou beholdest
But in his motion like an angel sings
Still quiring to the young-eyed cherubims
Such harmony is in immortal souls

William Shakespeare

Here lies Nolly Goldsmith, for shortness called Noll,
Who wrote like an angel, but talked like poor Poll.

David Garrick

The question is this: is man an ape or an angel? I am on the side of the angels.

Benjamin Disraeli

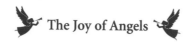

Oh woman! lovely woman! Nature made thee
To temper man: we had been brutes
without you;
Angels are painted fair, to look like you;
There's in you all that we believe of heaven,
Amazing brightness, purity, and truth,
Eternal joy, and everlasting love.

Thomas Otway

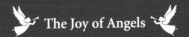

I saw the angel in the marble and carved until I set him free.

Michelangelo

Kind words are the
music of the world. They have
a power which seems to be beyond
natural causes, as if they were some
angel's song, which had lost its way
and come on Earth, and sang on
undyingly, smiting the hearts of men
with sweetest wounds, and putting
for the while an angel's
nature into us.

Frederick William Faber

 The Joy of Angels

Cease every joy, to glimmer on my mind,
But leave, oh leave the light of Hope behind!
What though my winged hours of bliss have been,
Like angel visits, few and far between.

Thomas Campbell

A SILVER ANGEL

On my birthday I was feeling sad because it was the third birthday I had spent without my son, Ed. He always made me feel special.

To take my mind off things, I decided to go the mall. I was walking across the parking lot when I spotted something shining on the ground. I looked down at it and felt this sudden urge to stop and pick it up. It was a silver angel. I turned it over and saw that it had Ed's birthstone on it.

I was shaken for a moment, and then a feeling of complete knowing came over me. My son was here. He had come to see me on my birthday. I had a silver chain around my neck that I very seldom wear. I put the angel on it and went on my way.

I thank God for the angel and this miracle. I thank Ed for remembering me. I felt blessed and peaceful that day. My son had let me know that he is always with me.

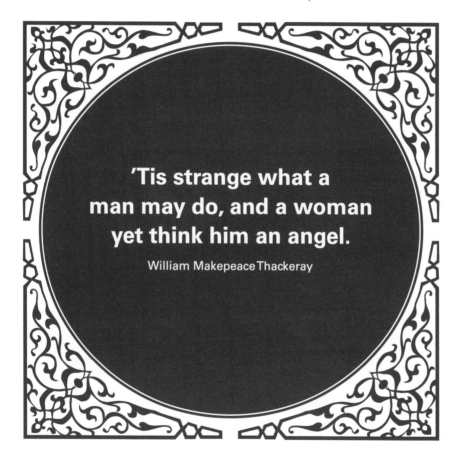

'Tis strange what a man may do, and a woman yet think him an angel.

William Makepeace Thackeray

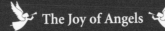
Happy those early days! when I
Shined in my angel-infancy,
Before I understood this place
Appointed for my second race,
Or taught my soul to fancy aught
But a white, celestial thought

Henry Vaughan

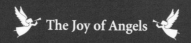

ON THE MOUNTAIN

Recently I was climbing a mountain in Wicklow on a very windy day with my son-in-law. As we neared the summit, there was a very strong breeze. We braced ourselves against it, but a severe gust of wind blew me off the track and I fell. My son-in-law tried to catch me, but to no avail. I rolled over and over, and then suddenly I stopped rolling.

My boot had got caught between two rocks and this is what stopped me. I had a severe pain in my ankle. I looked over my shoulder and saw behind me that there was a drop of about 15 feet onto large boulders. I was extremely lucky not to have fallen further. Although I had sprained my ankle, I would most likely have been severely injured, or killed, if I had fallen onto the rocks. My guardian angel was working overtime that day.

Angels descending,
bring from above,
Echoes of mercy,
whispers of love.

Fanny J. Crosby

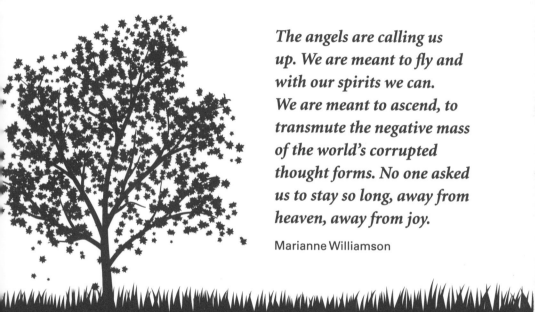

The angels are calling us up. We are meant to fly and with our spirits we can. We are meant to ascend, to transmute the negative mass of the world's corrupted thought forms. No one asked us to stay so long, away from heaven, away from joy.

Marianne Williamson